To Nevia,
You're a natural
Daymaker! Love,

Life as a Daymaker

Life
as a
Daymaker

HOW TO CHANGE THE WORLD
BY MAKING SOMEONE'S DAY

DAVID WAGNER

JODERE
GROUP
san diego, california

JODERE

GROUP

JODERE GROUP, INC.
P.O. BOX 910147, SAN DIEGO, CA 92191-0147
800.569.1002 • www.jodere.com

EDITORIAL SUPERVISION BY CHAD EDWARDS

The intent of the author is only to offer information of a general nature
to help you in your quest for emotional and spiritual well-being.
In the event you use any of the information in this book for yourself,
which is your constitutional right, the author and the publisher
assumes no responsibility for your actions.

Library of Congress Cataloging-in-Publication Data

Wagner, David.
    Life as a daymaker : how to change the world by making someone's day / by
David Wagner.
        p. cm.
Originally published: Minneapolis, MN : JUUT Press, c2001.
        ISBN 1-58872-075-6 (alk. Paper) -- ISBN 1-58872-076-4 (trade : alk. Paper)
        1. Kindness. 2. Benevolence. 3. Charity. 4. Humanity. I. Title.

BJ1533.K5W34 2003
177'.7—dc21

                                                              2002043477

                        ISBN 1-58872-075-6
                        06 05 04 03   4 3 2 1
                        First printing, April 2003
                        PRINTED IN CANADA

Book design by Charles McStravick

DAYMAKER *n.* A person who performs acts of kindness with the intention of making the world a better place.

Contents

Acknowledgments

I AM DEEPLY MOVED by the care, support, and nurturing that was bestowed on me through the process of writing this book. I express special thanks to the many people that have brought about this dream of tipping the scales within our lifetime to create love, joy, and harmony in the world. We live through simple deeds done with open loving hearts.

> To my wife, Charlie, for being my "way-shower." Your support and encouragement to live my truth is a blessing. Your love of life fills me up everyday.

> To my children, Coco and Ava, for being my teachers. Your sense of being, knowing, and unconditional love is a gift I cherish.

> To my parents for living a life that guided me toward writing this book. Your principle of giving to friends and strangers alike is a great legacy that has taught me so many simple truths.

> To my mentor, Horst Rechelbacher. Thank you for teaching me through your actions the values of passion, integrity, and unwavering commitment to your noble purpose.

To Anz Johansson, my dear friend. Your ability to take my words and help me express them with clarity gave me many insights because it made me think deeper and clearer as to the true purpose of *Life As a Daymaker*.

To each and every employee at Juut. I feel extremely fortunate to find myself surrounded by such beautiful people each day. Your dedication to being Daymakers and the love and joy you bring to our clients, and each other, feeds my soul.

To my friends in the publishing world who knew intuitively the potential of a Daymaker revolution. Vivian Glyck for discovering it, Patricia Gift for her insightful language, Arielle Ford and Brian Hilliard for finding the right partner in Jodere Group, and Debbie Luican of Jodere for living her life on purpose and supporting me in this dream. You have all become wonderful friends in the process.

Last and not least, to you, the reader: I thank you in advance for coming to this book. My wish is that you will be inspired to live *Life As a Daymaker*. In doing so, we can collectively create a ripple effect that will wash over humanity and create a world full of all that is good and right and true.

CHAPTER ONE

How Much of a Difference Can One Person Make?

*Let no one ever come to leave you
without leaving better and happier.
Be the living expression of God's kindness;
kindness in your face, kindness in your eyes,
kindness in your smile, kindness in your warm greeting.*

— MOTHER TERESA

IKE MANY, I SEARCHED FOR MY PURPOSE IN LIFE for quite some time. Happily, I have found that purpose in marrying my beautiful wife, Charlie, raising two beautiful spirited daughters, Coco and Ava, and sharing an idea I call "Daymaking" with everyone I touch.

I want to leave my children and others with an understanding of the impact they can have on society simply by caring for themselves, each other, and everyone in their lives. This is what I call Daymaking. To make someone else's day is truly soul's work that benefits everyone involved. A small act of kindness such as volunteering at your city's homeless shelter can feed individual souls and in turn nourish humanity. We also refill our own bucket every time we perform acts like these.

Many people don't know that "the best" in life includes serving others, so a sense of fulfillment eludes them. With Daymaking, I'm talking about genuinely making someone else's day. If you serve others for your livelihood, which many of us do, try serving wholeheartedly or with a "servant's heart." This does not mean with servitude, but with true care and compassion for the well-being of those you serve. Give 110 percent of yourself to make their day. It will elevate your work in doing so; I guarantee it, as long as it is thoughtful and genuine.

It does not take a lot of effort to be a Daymaker. Just behave in a caring way and watch what happens. Your life will begin to fill with perfect moments that serve the highest good of all. Perfect moments are not rare for a Daymaker. They happen all the time.

A LITTLE KINDNESS GOES A LONG WAY

*Never doubt that
a small group of thoughtful,
committed citizens can change the world.
Indeed it's the only thing that ever has.*

— MARGARET MEADE

IT ONLY TAKES A MOMENT TO MAKE SOMEONE'S DAY—to become a Daymaker—and sometimes those moments even change lives as I discovered a few years ago. I was working in my salon one day when a client came in to have her hair styled. I was surprised to see her since it was right in the middle of her five-week period between haircuts. I figured that she must have an important social engagement, so I asked her about her evening plans.

"I don't have anything special going on," she told me. "I just want to look and feel good tonight."

I gave her a great scalp massage, then shampooed and styled her hair. During our 30 minutes together, we joked and laughed. At the end, she smiled radiantly, hugging me goodbye.

A few days later when I received a letter from this client, I began to realize the enormous potential of Daymaking. My client admitted that she had wanted her hair styled so it would look good for her funeral. She had planned to commit suicide that very day. But the wonderful time she had during our appointment had given her hope that things could get better. She decided to check herself into a hospital and get professional help. She thanked me for caring, even though I hadn't known what she was going through.

I was stunned. I had spent time with this woman about once a month for three years, yet that day I had no inkling she was so distressed. I was glad to have made such a difference, but the experience left me with an enormous sense of responsibility. What if I had been upset, distracted, or hurried when she came to see me?

That experience made me take stock of myself as a stylist and as a person. How many of the ten clients I saw every day might be in a personal crisis that I would never have known about? Even if it were only one person a day, I might have no way of knowing who needed some extra attention. I resolved to treat every person I met like that woman. It might sound like a lot of work, but it wasn't hard to have fun with my client that day. It was natural and made my day brighter, too. I vowed to give care and attention to everyone I saw. I figured it would make their day a little better, and who knows, it might save a life.

I still thank my client for the gift of that letter because it changed my life as much as my kindness changed hers. When you realize the difference you can make for others, whether by spending a light-hearted half hour together, giving them a smile, or simply holding a door open for them, your whole approach to life shifts. Why have random acts of kindness when we can have intentional acts of goodwill?

We Can Change the World by Making One Day at a Time

Idealists . . . foolish enough to throw caution
to the winds . . . have advanced mankind
and have enriched the world.

— Emma Goldman

If we live with the intent of being Daymakers in everything we do, we will not only change our own lives, but the lives of everyone around us. This can have a powerful ripple effect. If I connect with ten customers in a day and they go on to connect with ten others that same day, together we have touched one hundred people. Our company services 4,000 people a day who each touch at least ten other people a day. That's 40,000 impressions a day or over 15 million a year. How many people do you see in a day? Now just imagine the opportunity we have to tip the scales of loneliness, suffering, and negativity that influence every person we meet.

How Did a Minnesota Farm Boy
Become a CEO with the Dream of Changing the World?

If you don't have a dream,
how you gonna have a dream come true?

– "Happy Talk"
from Rodgers and Hammerstein's *South Pacific*

When you grow up on a farm in rural Minnesota, the notion of doing something to change the world can seem far-fetched. But I was always industrious, curious, observant, and very conscious of people and their interactions. An average student, I sported primitive haircuts administered by my grandmother. Then at 14, I went to a professional salon for the first time. As rock music filled the air and beautiful women glided by, I decided to become a hairstylist.

During high school, I focused on this dream. I took accounting classes, figuring I would need to do the bookkeeping when I owned my own salon. I also took art classes to sharpen my creative skills.

When I graduated from high school, my father, a pipe fitter, asked what I wanted to do with my life. "I am going to be a hairstylist," I told him with conviction.

"No, you're not," he responded. "They don't make any money."

Realizing a Dream Is a Culmination of Small Moments

To be successful, the first thing to do is
fall in love with your work.

— Sister Mary Lauretta

Despite my father's objections, I held fast to my dream. After high school I found the best beauty school in Minnesota, the Horst Education Center (now the Aveda Institute). I was 18 years old, fresh off the farm, and ready to take on the world. Horst Rechelbacher, the owner, worked in the salon next to the Center and charged $100 for a haircut when the standard in most salons was about $12.

My first job after graduating from the Center was parking customers' cars at the main salon. And you know what? I did it really, really well. I did it so well that I made more money than some of the hairstylists. Eventually I got an "inside" job just in time to escape the coming Minnesota winter.

My position at the salon would best be described as "entry level." I shampooed clients' hair and folded towels. Again, I did it really, really well. Noticing my hard work and positive attitude, Horst asked me to be his personal assistant, which was a major turning point in my life.

As we worked together, Horst shared many intriguing stories about the hairdressing traditions of Europe. His stories were so enticing that I used the valet, shampooing, and assistant money I had saved to go to Europe and learn the techniques firsthand. I often worked for free to learn the secrets of the masters and had stints in some of the best salons in Europe.

When I finally returned to the U.S., Horst asked me to manage the St. Paul salon. He had started a product line called Aveda and needed to devote his full attention to it. Although the St. Paul location's revenue fell in last place among the company's four salons, I viewed it as a challenge and accepted the offer. The first time I saw the space, I knew I would either have to transform it, or never come back. You've probably guessed that I chose the former. The underutilized, but conscientious, employees were a big help. In my first week we had a pizza and beer night and cleaned the salon from top to bottom. Later, I brought in lively music and hip magazines and spent a lot of time training the staff. That year, our salon went from last place to first. The company named me both Stylist and Manager of the Year. Making over that salon was the

> *I saw how hope and initiative could change lives.*

start of my career as a Daymaker because I saw how hope and initiative could change lives. My persistence and ability to make the most of a situation was about to meet with a larger purpose.

When the vice president of the company resigned, Horst gathered the salon managers to get our input on filling the position. When it was my turn to speak I simply said, "If I were Vice President, I would work on education, marketing, and getting this place rocking!"

Two weeks later, Horst called me into his office. "The other day you told me what you'd do if you were Vice President," he reminded me.

"Yes, I did," I replied.

"Great. You're Vice President," he announced.

I didn't know how to run a four million-dollar company with 120 employees. But I did know how to attract, educate, and motivate great people. I jumped right into the job, a 23-year-old having fun at what he loved to do. I was making more money than I had ever dreamed of, living in a penthouse apartment, and enjoying my boat on the St. Croix River.

My younger brother turned 18 around that time. When my father asked what he planned to do, he said, "I'm going to be a pipe fitter, like you."

"Why don't you be a hairstylist?" Dad suggested. Times certainly had changed on the farm.

Through these experiences I learned that dreams or wild ideas could come true, in even more spectacular ways than you first imagined. You have not lived a perfect day until you have done something for someone without expecting them to repay you. We can experience the best in life by Daymaking.

FOLLOW YOUR DREAM

The important thing is this:
to be able at any moment to sacrifice what we are,
for what we could become.

— CHARLES DuBOIS

ONE DAY I NOTICED SOME AVAILABLE STOREFRONT SPACE in Uptown Minneapolis. I had dreamt of owning a salon since that first visit when I was 14. The travel, money, and prestige of working with Horst had kept my dream on the back burner for a while, but now I knew it was time to open a salon of my own.

Horst encouraged my independence. He thought that if I was successful, I could show others how to develop the Aveda concept outside of the company. It would have been easy to open with a full staff from the Horst Salons, but I don't believe in undermining your friends. What you put out into the world comes back to you. I started my new business, Salon Salon, with just two employees.

From the start we did things differently. We massaged the clients' scalp and shoulders before the shampoo, served espresso and Perrier, and played world music. Business was good and soon we were busy. We began hiring and training more students from beauty school. With all these expenses I sold the boat and moved into a studio apartment, paying myself $14,000 dollars a year each of the next three years. I toiled long hours and made many sacrifices during those lean years. But professionally I grew and laid the foundation for my future.

After the third year, the thriving business ran out of space. When Horst found out that I wanted to expand, he told me that he needed someone to run his salons. The Aveda product line had started to soar. We merged our salon companies and three years later I bought him out of the partnership. Since then, I have increased it to nine locations in the Twin Cities and bought Yosh Salon in Palo Alto, California, when famed hairstylist Yosh Toya retired. That acquisition kicked off our plan to expand nationally.

With the additional salons, we realized that we needed a new name—one that reflected our growing mission.

Our clients helped in the search for our new identity. One woman described her feelings about the essence of our company. "I give and I give and I give to my family, my work, and to my friends," she told us. "Here at this salon I get it back, so that I can go out and give it away again." We heard the same theme from other patrons.

That experience made me take stock of myself as a person.

Another described it as "having her bucket filled up." We liked the Japanese word Juuten, "to refill," so we decided to shorten it to "Juut," which as a first name means, "to uplift humanity and serve others." Juut captures the essence of our mission. Our commitment has paid off. Our company was recently voted one of the top 20 salons in the country and generates nearly $25 million in annual revenue. We have over 400 staff members/Daymakers, and we plan to expand around the country in the coming years. The heart of Juut lies in clarity, purity, and compassion. Creating a caring environment has not only made a better life for my clients and staff, but it has refilled my bucket many times over.

FOCUS ON YOUR WILD IDEAS

Nothing happens
unless first a dream.

— CARL SANDBURG

ABOUT 20 YEARS AGO, I STARTED FOCUSING ON MY WILD IDEAS after hearing a talk by motivational speaker Zig Ziglar. Now, every three months I write down all the things I dream of *being, doing, and having*. Sometimes, I come up with 50 things, other times 150. Over the years, I have written down: becoming President of the United States, driving a grand prix race car, living in the South of France, marrying the perfect woman, and being a famous actor to name a few. I suggest you give it a try, and don't just write down easy goals—stretch yourself with your wild ideas. Next, write in one sentence why you want to be, do, or have that particular goal. Then put the goals that have a clear purpose at the top of the list. Leave the others wherever they are on your list of wild ideas.

The next step is very important. Share your list with those who can help you realize your wild ideas. The more people you share your wild ideas with, the more likely they are to come true. Some of the wild ideas I have achieved include skydiving, racecar driving, and buying companies. Needless to say, I share ideas with everyone I know.

People get burned out easily if they don't achieve goals. Keep yourself away from burnout by constantly having purposeful actions. Working hard doesn't cause burnout, not achieving your goals does.

THE MOMENT I REALIZED I WAS A DAYMAKER

Life is a succession of lessons,
which must be lived to be understood.

— RALPH WALDO EMERSON

PART OF MY CAREER included doing styling demonstrations at hair shows around the country. Whenever I attended a show, I usually wore black leather pants. With my long hair, I looked like one of the guys from REO Speedwagon.

On one occasion, I had just finished with a show and was heading home. I boarded the plane and found my seat. I was next to a businessman dressed in a conservative suit and shiny wingtips. He gave me an odd look as I sat down next to him. I'm pretty sure he thought I was in the wrong section of the plane. Surely, I couldn't be flying first class at my age, and certainly not dressed like I was. Once the flight got under way he seemed to resign himself to the fact that we would be sitting together for several hours.

Closing my eyes, I mentally reviewed the seminar I had taught earlier that day. I had described to about 800 attendees the importance of not only doing great haircuts and colors, but the need to *make the day* of everyone who comes into our salons. Just then, the businessman decided to strike up a conversation by asking me what I did for a living. "I'm a Daymaker," I replied. "What in the world is a Daymaker?" he asked. "Well, I try to do something nice for another person every day. I call it Daymaking," I said with a smile. "You must do it very well," he added, apparently referring to my first class seat. I went on to tell him that I was a hairdresser, but that I "did hair" to make my client's day. He "got it" and so did I. From that day on, my business card has read: "David Wagner: Daymaker," instead of President/CEO. My clientele, business, and personal life improved dramatically after I became a Daymaker in every thing I did.

THE POWER OF KINDNESS

Remember that just so much are you adding to
the pleasure or misery of other people's days . . .
Whether each day of your life shall give happiness
or suffering rests with yourself.

— GEORGE MERRIAM

I WOULD LIKE TO SHARE THE POWER OF KINDNESS with more people. We all make an impact on the world around us, so why not use your power to make the world a better place? It's easier than you think.

For example, I had a client with thinning hair. Her mother and older sister also had thinning hair, but they chose to wear wigs. Connie was on the brink of getting a wig as well. Soon after I found out that she was receiving monoxidil treatments to reduce her hair loss, I spotted her in my waiting area looking frightened. All around her clients and staff with full, expertly styled hair chatted with each other, while photos of models with luxurious locks adorned the walls. There she sat in her own personal nightmare.

I greeted Connie with a smile, and sat her down in front of me. She glanced at me nervously, waiting for my assessment. "Is this your natural color?" I asked, looking her in the eye.

"Why yes it is," she replied surprised by my question.

"Wow, it's really pretty," I told her.

As she looked at me, her eyes welled up with tears. "You're the first person to compliment me on my hair in ten years," she confessed. Connie became my biggest fan and my best client, sending everyone she knew to me. "You've got to see David," she'd tell her friends. "He is such a nice guy." And they did by the dozens. All I did was notice something special about a person having a difficult time. Everyone has something beautiful about them. Why not point it out? Compliments don't cost you a dime to give, but can have unending value to the receiver.

BEAUTY TIPS

When I give, I give myself.

— WALT WHITMAN

AS A HAIRSTYLIST, I am constantly asked to offer advice about a person's hair—even if we've just met. The best beauty advice I have ever received did not come from a hairstyling master, or from a famous fashion designer, but from a client who gave me the following excerpt from the poem *Beauty Tips* by Sam Levenson. Her note said "David, this is something you have always intuitively known and shared with me without knowing you were."

> *For attractive lips,*
> *Speak words of kindness.*
> *For lovely eyes,*
> *Seek out the good in people.*
> *For a slim figure,*
> *Share your food with the hungry.*
> *For beautiful hair,*
> *Let a child run his fingers through it once a day.*
> *For poise,*
> *Walk with the knowledge you'll never walk alone.*
> *People, even more than things, have to be restored, renewed, revived,*
> *   reclaimed, and redeemed. Never throw out anybody.*
> *Remember: if you ever need a helping hand, you'll find one at the end*
> *   of your arm. As you grow older you will discover that you have*
> *   two hands. One for helping yourself, and one for helping others.*

She made my day by sending me this great poem, and by acknowledging that I lived by its message. There truly is beauty in everyone if you know where and how to look.

BEING KIND MAKES YOU HAPPY

We give because it feels natural and right.
We have taken our minds off our own troubles.
Self-pity and self-isolation no longer
dominate our thoughts.
We give for the sheer joy of giving
without the need for recognition.

— BRYAN ROBINSON

IF ALL OF THE ABOVE AREN'T REASONS ENOUGH to spread some kindness around, how about the most selfish reason of all? To be happy yourself. The joy of giving to another person has no equal. To know that someone else has been touched by our actions lifts our hearts. It shows us that our lives have a greater purpose than just getting a bigger house or a new car. When we give to others, we discover the greatest part of ourselves—our generosity.

CHAPTER TWO

To Make Someone's Day, Make Your Own Day First

Whoever is happy
will make others happy too.

— ANNE FRANK

MAKING SOMEONE ELSE'S DAY requires an open, joyful heart. To be inspiring, you have to feel inspired. It's unrealistic to expect yourself to feel generous towards everyone else if you routinely stumble out of bed, drink a cup of coffee, and then fight traffic while driving to work or dropping off the kids at school. You must fill your own cup first.

You can begin your day with any number of mood improving activities. I take immense pleasure in the little things. My daughters' laughs, giggles, and smiles help me daily to be in the moment and remind me that life is wonderful. You may find you like to start with some yoga or meditation to calm your mind. Or perhaps you'll want to experience the beauty of nature: listen to the birds outside, watch the rain falling, or catch the sunrise. Too many people start their day by watching TV or listening to negative drive-time radio. We choose how we begin and end each day so why not do it with something beneficial?

If you're stuck in a rut, getting out may be easier than you realize. Start by setting your alarm clock to go off 30 minutes earlier than usual. Then take this extra time to enjoy the morning stillness. My best inspirations requiring the least amount of effort come to me on these mornings. If you regularly take some quiet time, you may be surprised by what you discover about yourself.

If You Are a Car-Parker, Be the Best Car-Parker You Can Be

No one is useless in this world who lightens
the burden of it for someone else.

— Charles Dickens

My own story shows how you can make a difference in any job. The crucial piece is your attitude. If you love what you do, others will notice. And it will likely influence your destiny.

If I hadn't parked cars really, really well, I would not have gotten my inside job shampooing and folding towels.

Had I not shampooed and folded really, really well, I would not have been chosen to be Horst's assistant and gone to Europe.

Had I not gone to Europe, I would not have been able to make the changes in the St. Paul salon. Had I not made those changes, I would not have become Manager of the Year. Well, you get the idea.

The road to my success today began because I parked cars really, really well. Never believe a job is beneath you. Be the best at whatever job you have. It will make a difference in the world, and will prepare you for the road ahead. Wherever you are, be there.

Simplify Your Life and Reduce Stress

I believe that a simple and unassuming
manner of life is best for everyone,
best for both the body and the mind.

— Albert Einstein

Simplifying your life and reducing stress will give you more time and energy. Unfortunately, we often get so caught up in demands and schedules that we forget that our lives need only be as chaotic as we allow them to be. If you have many responsibilities, a number of the demands on your time may be unavoidable. But most of us have at least some commitments and relationships that we could let go of to make life more manageable.

I've found the following exercise helps me simplify when life's demands start to get out of control: Make a list of your highest priorities. Then make another list of the activities that support them. For instance, if being a good parent and spouse is a high priority, ask yourself what you can do each day to fulfill that goal. If being a kind person is also a high priority; put emphasis on activities that will support that as well. Next make a list of the people or activities that you find draining. Does being a highly scheduled overachiever bring peace and happiness to your family? Decide what kind of pace and activity feels the most comfortable. Schedule your life accordingly.

Since stress is a big energy drain, here are some simple suggestions for reducing it:

* ✳ Wake up and go to bed at the same time each day.
* ✳ Develop rituals such as baths or meditation to begin or end your day.
* ✳ Have dinner with your family, stay connected, and provide some stability.
* ✳ Watch the sunset.
* ✳ Take a walk in nature at least once a week.
* ✳ Turn your cell phone off before you enter your home.
* ✳ Wait to write e-mails until after the kids are in bed.
* ✳ Limit your use of technology: cell phones, pagers, and PDAs can create more stress and work.

Create Nurturing Surroundings

A peaceful home acts as a haven—a place for you to unwind and nourish yourself. Here are some suggestions for turning your home into a sanctuary:

* Create a family space as close to the kitchen as possible. Then your family can have conversations during meal preparation and clean up. Most of us spend 80 percent of our time here.

* Buy live flowers and replace them weekly. If you have a garden and flowers are in season, then pick some yourself.

* Fill your home with familiar scents that you find calming: candles, essential oils, and incense.

* Play soft music.

* Turn off the ringer on the phone during dinner and family time.

* Buy linens made from natural fabrics such as organic cotton. Use nontoxic cleaning products.

* Learn about Feng Shui—an Eastern concept of energy—and how it relates to your home. If you rearrange your furniture according to its principles, you may be surprised how different various rooms in your house feel.

* If you have a TV, keep it in an armoire or cabinet. Maybe if it's out of sight you'll watch less TV.

TAKE TIME FOR YOURSELF

> *Each person has his own safe place—running,*
> *painting, swimming, fishing, weaving, gardening.*
> *The activity itself is less important than the*
> *act of drawing on your own resources.*
>
> — BARBARA GORDON

WE ALL HAVE THINGS WE DO that make our hearts sing. Every day do something that makes you happy. You may love to write, dance, sing, ride your bike, do yoga, read the paper (or just the comics), cuddle, garden, or make pottery. In this case, what you love isn't as important as making time for it.

So choose an activity you love. Currently, how often do you do it? If not every day, why not? Make a promise to yourself to free up at least 15 minutes a day for your favorite activity. It could change your life.

Even the busiest person can find an extra 15 minutes a day. Here are some suggestions:

* Wake up 15 minutes earlier.

* Cut out 15 minutes of television time.

* Spend less time complaining or listening to someone complain.

* Cut down on extracurricular activities that you don't really enjoy.

* Make a place for your keys and *always* put them there
  (this can save 5–20 minutes).

* Do the same with your wallet or purse.

We all have activities that make us feel more joyful. Set aside time for them on a daily or, at least, a weekly basis. You owe it to yourself.

BLISS OUT ON A SPA NIGHT

How beautiful it is to do nothing
and then rest afterwards.

— SPANISH PROVERB

WHEN WAS THE LAST TIME you pampered yourself? A great way to recharge your batteries is to take a few hours in the evening to "spa out." Here is a very easy way to melt stress and refill your soul with good vibes. You will need the following:

* Favorite music, especially soothing sounds.
* A portable stereo.
* Candles scented with your favorite natural aroma.
* Bath salts/essential oils.
* Massage oil.
* Large bathrobe.
* A good book.
* Relaxing tea.

This may sound heavenly but impossible to you. If you have never taken this kind of alone time before, you might feel like it's a waste or an unattainable luxury. I cannot emphasize strongly enough that if you do not take care of yourself, you will not have much to give to others.

To get the most out of your Spa Night, make sure that you have two hours with no interruptions. Unplug the phone; put the kids to sleep, etc. Then run a hot bath, put on your favorite music, and light the candles. Next, pour bath salts and essential oils into the tub. Make a pot of tea and slide into your luxurious bath.

I recommend a breathing exercise while in the bath to help you get centered. Imagine drawing light into your heart when you inhale. Keep filling that space with more and more light. When you sense the stress leaving your body and light filling that space, you should feel more peaceful and inspired.

If you decide to shampoo your hair, take time to give yourself a scalp massage. Simply move your fingers around your scalp and forehead while massaging in a circular motion. Feel the sensation of stress melting away, especially around the temples. After your bath, massage your legs, arms, and shoulders. This will further relax your muscles. You can even use massage oil on yourself to make the massage smoother and easier. The Indian Ayurvedic tradition, which Horst taught me, recommends daily self-massage with essential oils.

If you do not take care of yourself, you will not have much to give to others.

Lastly, wrap yourself up in a large bathrobe, refresh your tea, and find a cozy place to read. I like poetry, but you should read whatever makes you feel peaceful and happy: books of inspirational quotes, a Victorian novel, or even a fashion magazine. However, I don't recommend reading newspapers, news magazines, or novels with a violent theme during this time. Remember, the idea is to create a little haven of calmness.

When I "spa out," I often feel more relaxed in just two short hours than I have on some week-long vacations. There is something especially nurturing about relaxing at home. Feel free to create your own rituals on your spa night. They might include taking time to write, sharing a foot massage with your partner, sitting in your garden or on your roof looking at the stars, stretching to soft music, walking in nature, or whatever else you enjoy.

NURTURE YOUR BODY, YOUR FOOD AFFFCTS YOUR MOOD

When eating,
eat

— ZEN MAXIM

EATING WELL IS ONE OF THE BEST WAYS to take care of yourself. Working with Horst from such an early age, I learned a lot about nutrition and the benefits of an Ayurvedic diet. For instance, uncooked fruits and vegetables are some of the healthiest, most energizing things you can eat. If you're skeptical about the role good nutrition plays in overall well-being, think about how you feel after you eat a fast food hamburger. Then consider how you feel after you eat a banana or a green salad. If you aren't aware of a difference, then try this experiment. Have a hamburger for lunch one day and pay close attention to how you feel afterwards. The next day have a large green salad and skip dessert, potato chips, or other processed foods. Notice how you feel this time. A simple diet really does give you more energy and a clearer mind.

Here are some more suggestions to get you in the habit of eating well:

✳ Avoid over processed foods. Instead buy organic produce and
   natural foods at health food stores and farmers' markets.

✳ Eat meals regularly. You'll be less likely to snack on potato chips,
   chocolate, or cookies if you do.

✳ Chew slowly and thoroughly. You'll digest your food more
   efficiently, and you'll feel fuller and more satisfied.

✳ Drink plenty of water—about eight 8-ounce glasses. It's the corner-
   stone of any healthy diet. When you examine what most of us
   drink—sodas, coffee, alcohol, and even fruit juices—none of them
   are as good for you as H_2O.

DEVELOP A YOGA PRACTICE

Health is the vital principle of bliss,
and exercise of health.

— JAMES THOMAS

YOGA IS INCREASINGLY POPULAR as more and more people discover how effectively it
calms their nerves, and tones their bodies. There are a number of ways to get
started, through books and videos, or classes in your community. Yoga classes are
popping up everywhere, so you may be surprised by what's available in your area.
My mother, who lives in a small Mid-Western town, takes classes at the senior
center.

EMPTY YOUR MIND REGULARLY

Peace does not dwell in outward things,
but within the soul.

— FRANCOIS DE FELON

IN THE PAST FIVE YEARS, HAVING A SPIRITUAL PRACTICE has become very important to me. I was greatly inspired by my friend Ray Civello, who spent time in India with some sadhus, or holy men, from the Himalayas. When he returned, he was a changed man. Seeing how Ray's soul had come alive, I realized just how much I didn't know.

Since I had too many responsibilities to make the same pilgrimage, I sought out resources closer to home. For example, I had gotten to know Dr. Justin O'Brien, author of *Walking with a Himalayan Master* and *The Wellness Tree*, and a celebrated American swami based in St. Paul, Minnesota. After listening to Ray's spellbinding stories, I told Dr. O'Brien that I wanted to learn what I didn't know. He chuckled, saying, "Ah, this time the student has arrived." We agreed to meet every Wednesday for two hours of meditation instruction. For the first three months, he just taught me to breathe correctly and intentionally. Before long others started to notice a change—I was more patient and understanding. Eventually I found myself meditating more deeply. Simultaneously my awareness of people and things around me increased.

The experience of meditation can be difficult to describe but the following example comes close. Imagine your mind is a lake. When the water is stirred by a storm, the mud from the lake's bottom clouds it up, making visibility difficult. Much of life is similar—there's a storm and the mud of activity and stress clouds our minds. Regular meditation helps keep your lake clear. The stormier life is, the more I meditate.

Surround Yourself with Great Role Models

*The most important single influence
in the life of a person is another person . . .
who is worthy of emulation.*

— Paul D. Shafer

I HAD A WONDERFUL UNCLE who lived into his nineties. At his funeral, his obituary card said, "Some people say that it's hell getting old, I was one of the lucky ones that got to." Live your life, share it with others, and be kind in every moment. If you do, getting old will be a pleasure. If you are young, find an older friend who can be your teacher and vice versa. Mitch Albom had Morrie Schwartz as his teacher and shared the wisdom Morrie imparted in his book, *Tuesdays with Morrie.* I have a friend and a soul mate in Gretta Freeman, a woman I first met as a client. When I was 26 years old, she asked me a question that I will never forget. "David," she said. "If you could have two words on your tombstone, what would they be?"

I thought about it while I cut her hair, and then told her I would let her know on her next visit. I gave this some serious thought and found that I couldn't quite capture it in two words. On her next visit, she asked if I had found my two words, "No, I couldn't find them," I had to tell her. "What are your two words?"

She looked me right in the eye, and with incredible wisdom said, "I lived." I was so taken by her answer that I asked her if I could borrow her two words. She and I have been the best of friends for nearly 20 years now. I no longer cut hair, so we regularly go out for lunch together. The lunches last for hours. Mitch had his Tuesdays; I have the great pleasure of "Wednesdays with Gretta." Whether it is a neighbor, client, or grandparent, we all have so much to share and gain from relationships with people outside our own generation. It's just as important for older people to befriend those much younger. Think how much better we'd all be if our society fostered relationships across generation lines. Everyone would benefit from a Gretta in his or her life.

LIVE TODAY, THIS IS NOT A REHEARSAL

For a long time it had seemed to me
that life was about to begin—real life.
But there was always some obstacle in the way,
something to be gotten through first, some unfinished
business, time still to be served, a debt to be paid.
Then life would begin. At last it dawned on me
that these obstacles were life.

— ALFRED D. SOUZA

THE 9/11 TRAGEDY JOLTED MANY AMERICANS into a sense of the preciousness of each day. None of us know how much time we have left. Too easily we let the days pass by as we count down to vacation, Christmas, or just the weekend. But every day is a precious gift, so live each one as if it's your last.

My first realization of how short life can be came when my sister, Michelle, passed away. She was 13, and I was 22. Born with what is referred to as a hole in her heart, at just a few months old, she was one of the youngest survivors of open-heart surgery. Michelle was an incredible kid. Although there were many things she couldn't do because of her condition, she was always smiling. Her cup was always at least half full. She gave me a priceless gift: the chance to know someone who was happy despite her circumstances, which included numerous surgeries.

When Michelle was 13, she arrived home from school one day, told my mother she didn't feel well and then went to lie down. When my mother checked on her a short time later, Michelle was gone. We later learned that she died of cardiac arrest. I still cannot imagine how difficult that must have been for my mother waiting for the ambulance, alone with my sister, and feeling helpless. It hits me especially hard now that I'm a parent. To endure the passing of a child must be one of life's most difficult challenges.

I remember a strange feeling recurring just after Michelle's death. I was grieving for Michelle and yet I still felt grateful and fortunate. My sister had survived multiple surgeries that could have ended her life. I also recall thinking, "What if that had happened?" I wouldn't have known what it was like to have a sister, particularly one as extraordinary as Michelle. Watching her celebrate her first birthday, when the odds were against her having another, and helping her learn how to twirl a baton and march around the garage, are among my favorite memories. Our family was blessed for 13 years with an incredible little girl of great spirit. Were it not for Michelle, my life would not be as full today. She did more, with grace and dignity; to give others hope than many people who live well into old age.

> *She gave me a priceless gift: the chance to know someone who was happy despite her circumstances*

When a loved one passes on, we remember the fragility of life and the importance of living in the present moment. Other events can have a similar effect. On a cool summer night, a few months after my daughter, Ava's birth, I was the keynote speaker for a local high school graduation. That night a student gave a speech that hit me like a two by four. I had been feeling sorry for myself—overwhelmed by all I was dealing with at home, in my business, and life in general. But this young woman's speech snapped me out of it and changed how I approach each day.

Here's what she said:

> *We convince ourselves that life will be better after we get married, have a baby, then another. Then we are frustrated that the kids aren't old enough, and think we'll be more content when they are. After that, we're frustrated that we have teenagers to deal with. We will certainly be happy when they're out of that stage. We tell ourselves that our life will be complete when our spouse gets his or her act together, when we get a nice car, are able to go on a nice vacation, when we retire. . . . The truth is, there is no better time to be happy than right now. If not now, when? Your life will always be filled with challenges. It's best to admit this to yourself and decide to be happy anyway.*

Her perspective helped me to see that, as the saying goes, "there is no way to happiness, happiness is the way." So, treasure every moment that you have, and do your best to make another person's day.

Remember that time waits for no one, so stop waiting until:

* You finish school.
* You lose ten pounds.
* You have kids.

* Your kids leave the house.
* You start work.
* You retire.
* You get married.
* You get divorced.
* It's Friday night.
* It's Sunday morning.
* You get a new car or home.
* Your car or home is paid off.
* It's spring, summer, fall, or winter.
* You're off welfare.
* It's the first or fifteenth.
* Your favorite song comes on the radio.
* You've had a drink.
* You sober up.
* You die.
* You are born again.

Decide that there is no better time than right now to be happy. Happiness is a journey, not a destination. When I am in the moment and being a Daymaker, that is when I feel my greatest happiness.

DANCE LIKE NO ONE'S WATCHING

We should consider every day lost
on which we have not danced at least once.

— FRIEDRICH NIETZSCHE

RECENTLY, I WENT TO AN OUTDOOR CONCERT by Taj Mahal, a rhythm and blues, jazz-fusion, musician who plays fabulous dance music. A little five-year-old girl and a man in his forties both danced very erratically in a group of people down near the stage. People around me cooed at how cute the little girl was, at the same time ridiculing the man for dancing so ridiculously in public. At what age does wholehearted enjoyment of music become goofy instead of cute? What if everyone danced like no one was watching? Some do. This man was enjoying his life. I admire those who feel secure and free enough to be themselves.

CHAPTER THREE

Make Your Mate's Day

We come to love
not by finding a perfect person,
but by learning to see an imperfect person perfectly.

— SAM KEEN

ALL MY LIFE, LOVELY WOMEN—from my mother, grandmother, aunts, and sister, to friends, coworkers, and clients—have surrounded me. I've had warm and loving relationships with them all. Still when it came to my personal life, I was not interested in settling down. Surrounded by so much beauty all day long, I never felt satisfied when I dated someone.

Then I met Shivnath. Shivnath Tandon came from India to work with Horst, and over time, we became friends. I enjoyed the stories he shared with me of his childhood in India and the lessons he learned from his swami. Over the years he watched me build my business and got to know my parents well. At one point they confided in him that while they were pleased with my success, they were concerned that I hadn't yet found the right woman. So Shivnath decided to tell me another story—this time about someone he knew from India.

Shivnath's friend came from a family that followed tradition and chose the wife for their son. Upon word that his father had found a match for him, the son announced that he wouldn't marry her. He wanted the perfect woman. "You have one year to find this perfect woman," his father told him. "If you do not, you will return and marry the woman I chose."

The son set off on his search. After a few months he called his father from London. "How is your search going?" the father asked.

"I have met the most beautiful woman I've ever seen," replied the son.

"She sounds perfect," his father said.

"No, we share no common interests, and she has no sense of humor," the dejected son admitted.

A few months passed and he called from Paris. He told his father of a new woman he had met. She was also from India and made him laugh constantly.

"She sounds perfect," the father commented.

"No, I'm not physically attracted to her at all," said the son.

The next time he called from Italy. "Father, you would not believe the woman I've met! She is incredibly attractive, and we love spending time together. We have everything in common, we even share the same thoughts."

"Well son, it sounds like you found the perfect woman. When will you marry?"

"Oh no Father," the son replied. "She has left me. She said she is looking for the perfect man."

Shivnath was trying to tell me that until I developed my whole self, not just my business side, I would meet the same fate. I don't know if this was a true story or a parable, but I got the message.

I met my wife, Charlie, on my twenty-ninth birthday at a party hosted by mutual friends. She had a great sense of humor and an infectious laugh. She also exuded confidence and wisdom that I found very attractive. I had met the perfect woman. However, it would take me five more years to become whole enough to consciously recognize my soul mate. Still I knew deep inside, that I had glimpsed my future that night.

THREE STEPS TO A HAPPY RELATIONSHIP

You cannot always have happiness,
but you can always give happiness.

— ANONYMOUS

ONE DAY I ASKED MY WIFE TO WRITE DOWN TEN THINGS that I could do to be a Daymaker for her. Here is her list:
What point do you think she was trying to make?

1. Listen
2. Communicate
3. Participate
4. Listen
5. Communicate
6. Participate
7. Listen
8. Communicate
9. Participate
10. Repeat 1-9

These three requests may seem simple, but they mean different things to different people. Do you really *listen, communicate, and participate?*

LISTENING

The only gift is a portion of thyself.

— RALPH WALDO EMERSON

WHEN ANOTHER PERSON IS TALKING, can you honestly say that you stop your own thoughts and follow what they're saying? Most of us listen to the beginning of what the other person says, then we begin formulating our response or thinking about something else all together. Even if we do pay attention to their words, we also need to be attuned to what those words mean to them. Our listening is usually filtered through our own life experience. Often we think of parallel situations or feelings we've had. Though this might seem like empathic listening, it can prevent us from truly understanding the other person's point of view. If we learn to listen attentively and without judgment we open ourselves up to a completely different way of seeing things.

COMMUNICATING

Learn the wisdom of compromise,
for it is better to bend a little than to break.

— JANE WELLS

IN THIS CONTEXT, it means asking for what you want and explaining why you want it. The other person need not agree with you. You may even agree to disagree. But if you ask for what you want, you are much more likely to get it. And if you explain why you want it, you will enjoy the benefit of being understood. You can avoid many problems in your relationship by simply stating your needs. Too often we assume that the other person should know what we want. We tell ourselves we would if we were in their shoes. But it's impossible to read their mind no matter how much you love them. So, if you want something, ask for it. Otherwise you have no one to blame but yourself.

PARTICIPATING

The quality of a life is determined
by its activities.

— ARISTOTLE

HAVE YOU EVER NOTICED how easy it is to be physically present in a relationship, while your attention is miles away? Don't even think you've given your loved ones quality time if you've been near them while watching TV, talking on a cell phone, or even reading. When Charlie and I are doing something together, I give it my undivided attention. If it's something that she loves and is better at than I am, I still find some part of it that I enjoy and can do well. For example, Charlie loves to cook and does it with panache while I don't have a clue about how best to combine ingredients or at what temperature to cook certain foods. But I'm a guy, so I love chopping things up with a knife. As Charlie works her culinary magic, I stand by her side, chopping everything she hands me. The same is true for gardening; while Charlie knows what to plant, I take great pleasure in digging big holes and pruning large trees and bushes.

To truly be considered quality time, participation requires meaningful inter-actions with your partner and loved ones.

EVEN SOUL MATES HAVE THEIR CHALLENGES

Nobody's family can hang out the sign,
"Nothing the matter here."

— CHINESE PROVERB

I CONSIDER MARRIAGE A 60/60 SPLIT because we should always give 10 percent more than we expect. Better still—don't expect anything. (I'm still working on that.) I enjoy my wife and our life together because I feel that she really is my soul mate. Soul mates know how to push buttons, make you think, frustrate you, challenge you, and love all your bumps and warts. I have grown immensely in my life through my marriage. I enjoy heated conversations and debates with my wife as much as the more peaceful times we spend together. We teach each other a lot and understand each other at a very deep level.

A successful marriage is one in which it never occurs to you that you've compromised anything.

SIMPLE GIFTS

A little thought and little kindness
are often worth more than a great deal of money.

— JOHN RUSKIN

ONCE CHARLIE AND I MARRIED, I learned something very quickly. Giving her a unique gift that cost one dollar meant more to her than a conventional and more expensive gift. On Valentine's Day a number of years ago, I was trying to figure out what I could buy that would let her know just how much I loved her. I walked in and out of many stores, clueless about what to get.

In the process I went to a drug store to get some cough drops. There, I saw a framed picture of a little boy and girl kissing on the beach. I bought the picture for $6.99 and went to a coffee shop to think about what I could write on it. At first, I simply wrote the name Charlie on a piece of paper and thought about our life together. Here is what I ended up writing on the photo:

Certain I would meet
Her someday, I kept looking.
All my life I knew what she would be like.
Rare as the most precious stone, yet she
Loves the little things in life: gardens, summer walks, and me.
I'm the most fortunate man I know.
Especially now with Charlie!

My poem on that picture is one of her most treasured possessions. It is easy to take for granted those who are nearest to us, or to acknowledge them with the obvious gifts that reflect how our society measures love. But it is so much better to find (or make) something from the heart that has special meaning. I know that was certainly the best seven bucks I ever spent.

IT'S THE LITTLE THINGS

I know some good marriages—
marriages where both people are just trying
to get through their days by helping each other,
being good to each other.

— ERICA JONG

EVERYDAY GESTURES OF KINDNESS remind your mate that you love them and think of them often. As the years progress, it becomes even more important to express your appreciation in new and unexpected ways that will help maintain the wonder and magic of your relationship. Here are a few ways to make your partner's day.

* Compliment them in public as well as in private
* Leave love notes on the bathroom mirror to start their day
* Put a love note in a place where they will find it sometime during the day: briefcase, wallet, car, coat pocket, etc. Even if they don't find it for days, it will still make their day when they do

* Send flowers anonymously, for no reason at all except that you love them dearly
* Hold hands in public and act like you're dating even if you've been together for a long time

TELL THEM YOU APPRECIATE THEM OFTEN

Love is how we feel toward those who show us
that which is lovable about ourselves.

— GERRY SPENCE

IN OUR BUSY LIVES it's easy to focus just on what needs to get done each day. When we live with someone, especially if you have children, the to-do list can become the main topic of conversation. So, it's important to remember how lucky you are to have this person in your life. Everything they do for you is out of a desire to make your life together better. They don't have to be there. They do things for you because they love you and want to support you. At any moment they have the option to go start a life elsewhere. Plenty of people do. But instead, they stay. Even if life with them isn't always easy, look closely at what they bring to the relationship. Does she keep the house clean, take care of the children, or cook meals for you frequently? Do you have any idea how much work this is? Does she pick up your dry cleaning or pay all the bills? Does he take care of the yard or the car? Does she work outside the home despite all that she does for the family? Does he always remember to put a glass of water on your bedside table at night? How many things does your mate do that you don't thank them for?

Well, thank them. Often. Tell her how much you love the way she cares about others. How she buys birthday cards for every member of your family and makes sure they're in the mail on time. Tell him how you love his eyes, or his smile. These little things often get lost in our day-to-day lives. We can forget to stop and really take in this wonderful person who walks through this life with us. They do so much, and if one day they weren't there anymore, you will wish you had told them you appreciated them more.

LEARN MASSAGE, PRACTICE FREQUENTLY

The most exquisite pleasure
is giving pleasure to others.

— JEAN DE LA BRUYERE

MASSAGE IS A WONDERFUL WAY to nurture your partner—it gives you the chance to express your love nonverbally—and it enhances their well-being, both physically and emotionally. There are a number of videos and books that teach massage. Find one and then practice on each other regularly. Have fun by experimenting with different techniques and massage oils. Honor your partner by letting them enjoy the massage without having to immediately reciprocate. Often it's nice to give each other a massage on different nights. Then the person who has just received doesn't have to give up their state of relaxation.

REMEMBER THEY'RE SPECIAL

The more I wonder ...
the more I love.

— ALICE WALKER

WHEN WE SPEND EVERY DAY WITH SOMEONE, it's easy to lose sight of what makes him or her special. Once they've unclogged the toilet and suffered a few bouts of the stomach flu, much of their mystery is lost, which can lead to trouble in many long-term relationships. The beauty of your partner isn't in exquisitely chiseled abs or perfectly applied make-up. The wonder of them doesn't lie in anything physical, but in the magic of their soul. Never think you know someone completely. There are likely many unique things about them you have yet to discover.

CHAPTER FOUR

Make Your Child's Day

My best creation is my children.

— DIANE VON FURSTENBERG

BECAME A GROWN UP the moment my oldest daughter, Coco, let out her first cry. Many roles are easy to adopt and discard, but once you have a child you will never *not* be a parent. They are yours to care for, to teach, and to cherish. They are our most precious charges and it's our responsibility to help them fulfill all of their potential.

My wife and I have been blessed with two incredible children. Our first daughter, Coco Arabella, and our second, Ava Mirabella, are six and four years old. The lessons I've learned thus far in fatherhood have served many other areas of my life. The understanding, patience, compassion, and lessons I have gained from my children have all helped me to be a better boss, friend, brother, and son.

Fathers need to get to know their children as thoroughly as mothers do, and it's never too early to start. By having their father talk to them in the womb, children will associate the same sense of comfort from their father's voice as they do with their mother's voice. In the womb they will respond to your voice by kicking and moving around. You can make their days even before they are born.

When my wife gave birth to our first daughter we briefly cuddled her before the nurses took her to be weighed, cleaned, and documented. Fathers can take this opportunity to bond with their child. Instead of sitting behind a glass wall videotaping your baby, roll up your sleeves and give your child its first hugs. From the second they are born, show them the indescribable love you have for them. You will carry the memory forever and they will hold the imprint of being lovingly welcomed into the world.

When my wife, daughter, and I came home from the hospital, my mother-in-law and sister-in-laws offered to help our transition. Quickly I found myself in the background taking care of household logistics instead of Charlie and Coco. Even after hours of birth and parenting classes, I felt ill-prepared and unnecessary those first few days.

One evening as I sat rocking my new daughter, I began thinking about how I could make her day. Finally, it dawned on me: massage.

One evening as I sat rocking my new daughter, I began thinking about how I could make *her* day. Finally, it dawned on me: *massage.* So that week I took Coco to one of our spas to have a massage therapist teach me how to work on her tiny body. I also bought a how-to book on infant massage. From then on, I gave Coco a massage every night at exactly the same time. It became a ritual that allowed me to bond with her in a tender, comforting way.

Mothers also need lots of care. Foot and back massages are gifts she can look forward to at the beginning or end of the day. There are some wonderful videos on pregnancy massage that also helps both parents to bond with this new little person. My wife's friends envied her when she told them about our massages, baths, and other rituals during and after her pregnancy. Make your wife's day! Every day! All it takes is some soft music, a little massage oil, and a couple of soothing Daymaker hands.

WRITE POEMS ABOUT THEM WHEN THEY'RE BORN

Kind words can be short and easy to speak,
but their echoes are truly endless.

— MOTHER TERESA

I WAS VERY LUCKY to be able to spend a lot of time at home with my new family. I learned so much during the first month of Coco's life. At only a few weeks old, her spirit, will, and character were very evident. Because I had gotten to know her right from the start, I was better able to nurture her potential. I highly recommend that parents take the time to enjoy the precious moments of this new life.

Here is Coco's Birth Announcement:

Announcing the birth of
Coco Arabella Wagner
Born to David and Charlie Wagner
On September 30, 1996
Weighing 6 pounds, 10 ounces
and measuring 19 inches long.

Complete is the word most
Often in my mind when I look at her.
Children have always had me in the palms of their hands,
Ours has me to the tips of my toes and more.

Already she
Reaches out to touch the smiling faces of everyone
Around her.
Before we know it, these little hands will
Explore, discover, finger paint, and play the piano.
Little hands that may someday sculpt, cut hair, or heal those in pain.
Love has never meant more to me
And everyday I can only hope I'm worthy of this blessing we call Coco.

— HER FATHER

Writing a personal announcement gave me a chance to capture the magic and awe I felt. I know it will mean so much to her when she is older. If anything ever happens to me, she will know that I recognized her essence, her soul, and her potential.

LOVE THEM UNCONDITIONALLY

There is nothing more thrilling in this world,
I think, than having a child that is yours,
and yet is mysteriously a stranger.

— AGATHA CHRISTIE

OUR SECOND DAUGHTER, Ava, came along when we had just purchased our salon in California. About four months into our highly leveraged deal, while we were in contracts, remodeling, hiring, and training a new staff, we found out Charlie was pregnant. We were already trying to figure out how to get half way across the country with one 18-month-old child, and now we would have an infant too.

My travel demands made it difficult to give Charlie the same support as I did with our first child. But I did my best. In the middle of Charlie's second trimester, our doctor discovered a possible abnormality. The test revealed that the baby had a high risk for Downs Syndrome, Spina Bifida, or a combination of other birth defects.

How could I possibly make Charlie feel better after that news? I could only offer silent strength. We drove home tightly holding onto each other's hands. When a song sung by the Italian opera singer, Andrea Bocelli, came on the stereo, its beauty struck us both so deeply we fell silent. We listened to that same song over and over, into the night, and later on our way to other doctor's appointments; anytime we just wanted to share that moment. To this day, when we hear it, we cry.

We went to many meetings with doctors and genetic counselors, who tried to prepare us for the worst, while suggesting we hope for the best. They told us that to have a conclusive diagnosis, they would need an amniocentesis. We wanted to know what we faced, so we could emotionally prepare ourselves, research the issues, and welcome this exceptional spirit into our lives.

During the amnio, the monitor showed the needle enter Charlie's womb and our child reach out for it with her tiny hand. Twelve days of anxiety followed. The prayers and love from our family and friends kept us going. This support gave us the confidence that we could deal with any outcome. "If not us, then who?" I asked my mother late one night. "We can handle this emotionally, spiritually, and financially. We can do this, and we will."

Finally, we found out that our baby was healthy. Although there could still be some unforeseen complications, it appeared the immediate danger was gone. I felt a mix of gratitude and relief that we would have a normal child. Yet somehow, I had a strange sense of loss of the lessons we would have learned from a child with special needs.

> *We wanted to know what we faced, so we could emotionally prepare ourselves, research the issues, and welcome this exceptional spirit into our lives.*

On February 20, 1999, our daughter, Ava Mirabella, was born healthy but sporting a perfectly round birth mark the size of a silver dollar on the crown of her head with a two inch long, pitch black crop of hair growing out of it. We were amazed at our Little Buddha.

When we brought Ava home, a friend of ours said, "This birthmark is where God put his hand on her when you accepted her however she may be." In her short life, she has taught me more than anyone else. She brought us fear, hope, and unconditional love. We have another wise little Daymaker in our lives.

Again, each night I performed infant massage on my new daughter. I wanted to express my appreciation to her for the lessons she taught us and to God for placing her in our lives.

Here is Ava's Birth Announcement:

Announcing the birth of
Ava Mirabella Wagner
Born to David and Charlie Wagner
On February 20, 1999
Weighing 7 pounds, 7 ounces
and measuring 19½ inches long.

Again I am reminded of the
Very greatest gift of all—the unconditional love of
Another.

Mere words simply can't describe her will and spirit.
In God we trusted and here we are today looking into her eyes,
Reveling in what we have to share with this world.
Already she inspires us to
Be all that is good and right and true.
Everyone will notice these
Lovely lips, as they will speak words of kindness, these
Lovely eyes, as they will seek out the good in all people.
And everyday I will hope I am worthy of this blessing we call Ava.

— HER FATHER

WRITE A FAMILY MISSION STATEMENT AND LIVE IT

You've got to think about big things
while you're doing small things,
so that all the small things go in the right direction.

— ALVIN TOFFLER

SO MUCH IS MADE OF MISSION STATEMENTS in business. Yet in our private lives, we seldom pause long enough to identify what is important to us as individuals, much less as a family. My wife and I share strong beliefs and values. Years ago, we sat down and developed a Family Mission Statement that defines those shared beliefs and values. I encourage you to create your own. If you need help, Stephen Covey's book, *The 7 Habits of Highly Effective Families*, can guide you.

The Wagner Family Mission Statement

We are a loving family that nurtures each other, as well as, our community of friends and family. We enthusiastically share our life experiences. We believe that love is unconditional and that trust and respect are earned. We give thanks through meditation and prayer and recognize all that we have been blessed with. We value our health of mind, body, and spirit. We nurture our minds with education, experiences, and lifelong learning. We nurture our bodies with exercise and by eating excellent foods. We nurture our spirits by meditating, nurturing others, and expressing our love for each other.

KEEP A DIARY FOR THEM

*I'm always fascinated
by the way memory diffuses fact.*

— DIANE SAWYER

EVERY YEAR IT AMAZES ME how many little and big things about our children's experiences I forget. I decided when Coco was about to celebrate her first birthday that I would write her a letter recounting the year. I shared the things she's taught me, how much I love her, and what she's added to my life. I now write a letter on each birthday my daughters celebrate. I put the letter in a special envelope, seal it, and put it in our safe. I intend to give them their letters on their eighteenth birthdays. I pray I am around to be there when they read them, and if I'm not, I will have the comfort of knowing I expressed how I felt about them.

CHILDREN SPELL "LOVE": T-I-M-E

*What feeling is so nice as a child's hand in yours?
So small, so soft, and warm, like a kitten
huddling in the shelter of your clasp.*

— MARJORIE HOLMES

YOU KNOW HOW MY KIDS SPELL "LOVE"? It's T-I-M-E. Not only the quantity of time, but also the quality of it. Finding activities that you share regularly with your children is an important part of parenthood. Flying kites, baiting a hook to go fishing off the end of the dock, riding a bicycle, and taking long walks on the beach looking for shells are some of our favorites. Time is not money, although some people maintain it is. Time is life. I believe my children will judge me by the time we've spent together, not by how much money I've made. Make your kids' days by giving them a part of yours. Spending time with your children is a gift to you both.

CREATE A QUIET, PEACEFUL HOME

The ability to concentrate
and to use your time well
is everything.

— LEE IACOCCA

TEACH YOUR CHILDREN the joy of quiet and solitude. This will allow them time to develop their own thoughts instead of being bombarded by someone else's through TV, video games, or even their friends. Cultivating peaceful and alone time will help your child learn to concentrate, use her imagination, and feel happy by herself. It will help her mentally and emotionally for the rest of her life.

PLAY

> *He who does not get fun and enjoyment*
> *out of every day . . . needs to reorganize his life.*
>
> — GEORGE MATTHEW ADAMS

GO TO THE PARK and have some fun. I used to go with the kids and just watch them play. Eventually I found that I got more out of it by becoming a child myself and playing on the monkey bars. I can tell you that my kids get more out of it as well. Life is more enjoyable if you spend less time as a spectator on the sidelines.

SPEND TIME IN NATURE

> *Climb the mountains and get their good tidings.*
> *Nature's peace will flow into you*
> *as sunshine flows into trees . . .*
> *while cares will drop off*
> *like falling leaves.*
>
> — JOHN MUIR

MAKE A RITUAL of watching sunsets with your children. We are fortunate to live on a lake, so we regularly find a quiet place to just anchor our boat and be with each other during this magical time of day. Don't live near a lake? It's just as easy to set up a blanket in the back yard or your favorite park. By connecting with nature, your child will develop an appreciation for the environment and an ability to enjoy the simple gifts in life. Of course, memories of sharing such moments with you will stay with him forever.

LAUGH OFTEN AND AT YOURSELF

The most thoroughly wasted of all days
is that on which one has not laughed.

— NICOLAS DE CHAMFORT

LAUGHTER LIGHTENS OUR MOODS and bonds us to others. By laughing with your child, you will show her a flexible, lighthearted way to deal with stress, disappointments, and change. And, most importantly, it will bring happiness to you both. Be sure to laugh at yourself, as well. This can show her how to accept and move past her own mistakes. Laughter is a tool she will use for the rest of her life.

UNDER PROMISE AND OVER DELIVER

If parents keep their promise to [their child],
[he] will learn to trust in them, in himself,
and in long-range payoffs.

— STEPHANIE AND ROBERT PRESSMAN

TO A CHILD, AN ADULT, ESPECIALLY A PARENT, is a powerful figure, a symbol of authority. Children depend on adults for many things: love, time, material needs, and their sense of self. So if you promise your child you'll play soccer or go fishing, the child will eagerly gather their equipment and wait for you. If you promise to bring them a toy or take them to Disneyland, they will pin their hopes on it. If you forget or get too busy, a child feels her disappointment deeply. By keeping your promises, you help your child to feel valued and to trust you in return. As a parent I now make fewer promises, so I can keep them all. My six-year-old coaches me on this daily. A promise is sacred to a child. Make it sacred to you, too.

NEVER PASS UP A MOMENT TO SHOW THEM LOVE

The giving of love is an education in itself.

— ELEANOR ROOSEVELT

PARENTS KNOW THAT CHILDREN are our most precious treasures. Life gets busy and it can be easy to race from one responsibility to the next. Make hugging your children and telling them you love them a part of your day. Write them notes, leave them messages, and blow them a kiss. Throughout the day, show them you love them in every way you can. A child can never feel loved too much. Your love creates the foundation for how they feel about themselves and their abilities for the rest of their lives.

DON'T BRING WORRIES HOME FROM THE OFFICE

Worry is like a rocking chair.
It will give you something to do,
but it won't get you anywhere.

— THE UNITED CHURCH OBSERVER

WHEN YOU WALK IN TO GREET YOUR FAMILY, ROOMMATE, OR SPOUSE, leave the garbage outside. Imagine there is a hook outside your door where you hang all your troubles and worries for the evening. I have noticed that when I do this, there always seems to be fewer of them when I leave the next morning.

BE A DAYMAKER TO TEENAGERS

The world was not left to us by our parents;
it was lent to us by our children.

— AFRICAN PROVERB

THE TEEN YEARS are an important transition to adulthood. It can be confusing to parents to try to figure how to relate to a child who suddenly wants so much independence. If your teenagers seem distant and difficult to connect with, remember that they still need you very much. Your approval will always matter, even if for a few years they pretend it doesn't.

Here are a few ways to make the day of an adolescent, whether with your own child or someone else's.

1. *Compliment them on anything positive that you can.* Teenagers these days often have enormous responsibilities. Even if they don't appear to, people in this age group still crave their parents' approval. They benefit from admiration as much as anyone. Be generous in your praise, especially praise for compassionate, responsible behavior. This will create a happy, healthy adult more readily than nagging them.

2. *Encourage them to give their time to help others.* Another part of becoming an adult is learning how to personally impact the world. Show them how to make a difference to others. It will help them create a positive self-identity. They will feel good about themselves, have a stronger connection with others and feel that they belong to the community.

3. *Be there for them.* Adolescents must sort through issues from their looming adulthood to intense peer pressure. They may not always feel comfortable sharing these struggles with someone older, but if you create a safe place where they can discuss bigger issues with you, it will help them. Tell them about some of your difficulties as a teenager to open up the communication. Most importantly, let them know that you care about them and will help them through anything.

TELL THEM THEY CAN DO ANYTHING

The greatest good you can do for another
is to not just share your riches,
but to reveal to him his own.

— BENJAMIN DISRAELI

WHAT WE CREATE WITH OUR LIVES reflects what we believe we can do. We are only limited by our dreams. Even the greatest achievers have stories riddled with skeptics and naysayers. Other people may tell your children what they cannot do. Don't be one of them. Many of the most successful members of society recall that their parents told them they could accomplish anything. Tell them that anything is possible and that they have the power to change the world. By instilling this belief in your children, you will give them strength and confidence to draw from during their greatest challenges. Encourage them to tell you their wild ideas. Help them accomplish their dreams.

CHAPTER FIVE

Make Your
Whole Family's Day

Family faces are magic mirrors.
Looking at people who belong to us,
we see the past, present, and future.
We make discoveries about ourselves.

— GAIL BUCKLEY

T HESE DAYS MOST PEOPLE HAVE BUSY LIVES and may not see their extended families as often as they would like. We can still reach out to these loved ones in simple, but powerful ways. Following are some ideas to get you started.

Remember Birthdays

Acknowledging family members' birthdays shows them that they are in your heart and your thoughts. A phone call on someone's birthday can tell them they are special to you. Make a point of marking all family members' birthdays in your calendar or enlist the help of someone who is good at keeping track of these things to remind you. My mother keeps me posted since I'm not good at staying on top of these dates.

Send Cards and E-mails

What a wonderful thing is the mail,
capable of conveying across continents
a warm human hand clasp.

— RANJAN BAKSHI

Technology makes it easier than ever to keep in touch with distant relatives, even if we don't have the time for a long phone conversation every week. Send them e-mails regularly, even just brief updates of your life and ask questions about theirs. If you like to forward e-mails, write a personal note at the top for the person you're sending it to. Occasionally, sending cards by snail mail is another great way to make someone's day. Tell them you've been thinking about them or just remind them of a funny experience or joke you shared. These little touches express the love that families long for from each other.

> *If you like to forward e-mails, write a personal note at the top for the person you're sending it to.*

One member of my staff told me that she gave the first edition of this book to her 84-year-old grandfather on Christmas. A generally unexpressive man, he surprised the entire family by reading the book, and then on New Year's Day presenting his wife with a poem about how much he appreciated her. The grandmother called various family members all day long weeping tears of joy. It meant so much to her to have this expression of love from her husband. Gestures like this, from those dearest to us, become our most precious memories.

Send Your Parents Flowers on Your Birthday

Gratitude is the memory of the heart.

— J. B. MASSIEU

Your birthday is a special day for you, but it was also a special day for your parents, who remember it much better than you do. Take the time to make your birthday wonderful for the people who made it possible. Expressing gratitude will bring you even more joy on your birthday.

Focus on the Positive in Them

*We awaken in others the same attitude of mind
we hold toward them.*

— ELBERT HUBBARD

Family members know each other better than anyone. You've seen one another through many ups and downs. Even though not all families are ideal, each has good in them. Whether you see your extended family often, or just every year or two, focus on the good things about them. Be especially kind to each other, since people can be more sensitive to their families' approval. Tell them what you like and admire about them. Respect and appreciation for their talents can heal relationships. It's important to have the boundaries you need for your own happiness, but focus on the positive as much as you can. Upbeat letters, cards, and e-mails can keep those connections in a way that makes everyone's days.

GRANDCHILDREN

Grandparents . . . sprinkle stardust
over the lives of little children.

— ALEX HALEY

GRANDPARENTS PLAY A NOBLE ROLE. Since they don't have to be the disciplinarians, they can unconditionally love and nurture a child, which helps build character and confidence. The connection between grandparent and grandchild can be magical. Grandparents get to pass on legends, folklore, family trees, songs, and nursery rhymes from previous generations. Stories from their youth or their own parents' childhood will stay with them their whole lives. Our kids are fascinated with reminiscences of celebrating Christmas, working on the farm, or going fishing. It amazes me how many times they want to hear the same story over and over. Here are some more suggestions for making the most of your role as grandparent:

* Play games with your grandchildren that may be unfamiliar to them. Perhaps they will teach them to their own children one day.

* Children love mail, so send your grandchild a letter in the mail even if you live nearby and see them frequently.

* Find an outdoor activity all of you enjoy, such as flying a kite in the summer or sledding in the winter. My parents have a little hill in their backyard where we toboggan. To my daughters, that little hill is their very own mountain. My parents sit behind them and make all kinds of noise while going down the hill and my daughters talk about it for months.

* Give your grandchild a hug and a kiss instead of asking them for one.

* Telephone your grandchild regularly, and let them know you're calling especially to speak with them.

* If you live too far away to frequently see your grandchildren, videotape yourself reading a bedtime story for them.

* Dress up with your grandchildren. My mom has a collection of hats that the girls love to get into when they visit. They have even made an occasion of it and wear them out to a restaurant.

* Keep a wall chart where you document how much they have grown.

* Go to their recitals and class plays, and give them flowers afterwards.

* Write a letter to your grandchildren on their birthdays. Put it in a safe place to be given to them when they're older.

* Ask their parents if you can participate in various rites of passage, such as taking them:
    * To the zoo
    * For their first haircut
    * Shopping for clothes and supplies for the new school year
    * To buy their first bike/skateboard/pair of skates
    * To buy their first razor
    * To their first make-up lesson/facial
    * Out to their first movie

* To eat sushi or some other new food
* To their first play or concert

Family ties are among the most important connections we have. Remember to reach out to those you love in caring and creative ways. It will brighten their day and strengthen your connection to them.

CHAPTER SIX

Make a Friend's Day

. . . I have learned that to have a good friend
is the purest of all God's gifts,
for it is a love that has
no exchange of payment.

— FRANCES FARMER

OUR BEST FRIENDS ARE KINDRED SPIRITS we've been fortunate to meet along the way. They are there to lean on when we need them, and we are there for them in kind. They're understanding when we are busy, and when we get together after a long absence, there is still a comfortable rapport. Best friends are treasures and we need to make sure they know how much they mean to us. What better way than making their day?

Offer Support When They Need It

Everyone needs help from everyone.

— Bertolt Brecht

We all go through challenging periods, such as when Charlie and I faced the possibility that our daughter could have a birth defect. These are the times when we need all the support we can get from friends or loved ones. Prayers, understanding words, and a listening ear go a long way. Sometimes a friend might need you to just sit quietly and listen while they express their feelings. In other circumstances, you may be able to help in concrete ways, such as bringing a meal, taking care of their children for a night or weekend, or by some other small but thoughtful act. Most importantly, let your friends know that you are there for both their triumphs and their challenges. The presence and support of friends acts like loving hands that give us courage and hope to grow and move forward. Be the kind of friend to someone that you would want to have yourself.

Give Them Space When They Need It

Often we can help each other most
by leaving each other alone.

— Elbert Hubbard

Sometimes we enthusiastically want to help people who want nothing more than some time alone. Perhaps they need to grieve, plan, or contemplate events on their own. If you notice that someone around you has become withdrawn, reach out and ask them if you can help in any way. If they say no, assure them that you are available should they need you, then back off. Sometimes respect and privacy are the best Daymakers of all.

REMEMBER BIRTHDAYS

The whole worth of a kind deed
lies in the love that inspires it.

— THE TALMUD

BIRTHDAYS ARE IMPORTANT in our culture because they provide an opportunity to celebrate how special a particular person is to us. Though, as adults we grow out of thinking the world stops for our birthday, it still means so much when friends remember. Celebrating someone's birthday is a simple way of telling them that they matter and you love them. As I mentioned earlier, I have never been very good at keeping birthdays straight, but because I know how important it is, I welcome coaching from those around me.

End Phone Calls with "I Love You"

There is only one happiness in life,
to love and be loved.

— George Sand

It is wonderful to connect with the people we care about, and the telephone is an easy way to do just that. Ending a call with "I love you" reminds them of how special they are to us. Most people love the pick-me-up of hearing those words. Nowadays I hear those words more often between friends and it always makes my day.

Help Them Fulfill Their Wild Ideas

If you can dream it,
you can do it.

— Walt Disney

Back when I was single, I kept my list of wild ideas on my refrigerator. One day my roommate woke me up by announcing that he was going to make one of my wild ideas come true. That was my first and last skydiving trip. As I mentioned before, the more people you tell about your dreams and wild ideas, the more likely they are to come true. Be sure to return the favor. When you make someone's wild idea come true, you have a friend for life.

E-MAIL AND FAX ARTICLES THAT REMIND YOU OF THEM

Hold a true friend with both of your hands.

— NIGERIAN PROVERB

WE ALL HAVE MOMENTS during the day when something we see reminds us of a friend or family member. Instead of just turning the page or forgetting it, clip that article or cartoon and put the person's name on it, or e-mail it to them. If you see a film or show you think someone special would enjoy, send them a quick e-mail to tell them about it. These personalized contacts don't take long and they let your friends know that they are in your thoughts, even if you don't speak very often. Such contacts can make their day with a laugh, an insight, or important bit of information. It expands their experience and keeps you connected with the people you love. Even though lives get busy, it makes our days to know someone special is thinking of us.

Friends are a treasure and blessing in our lives. We can make their days in an endless number of ways. Laugh, care, always be there, and you will be the best friend they can have.

CHAPTER SEVEN

Make a Stranger's Day

The best portion of a good man's life—
his little nameless, unremembered
acts of kindness and love.

— WILLIAM WORDSWORTH

W HEN WE GO OUT IN THE WORLD to get things done, we come into contact with countless strangers. From time to time we may ask ourselves, "Who are these people and why are they always in my way?" It's important to remember that we are all strangers to someone. How would you like the frazzled cashier at the grocery store to treat you when you realize that you forgot that one all important item and would like to add it to your bill, even though she's already totaled it? I'm fairly certain that you'd like her to understand. Each of us knows the huge effort it can take to extend this sort of kindness or benefit of the doubt to a family member. The next test is to give that same benefit to a stranger.

REMEMBER: YOU DON'T KNOW THE WHOLE STORY

Be kind.
Everyone you meet
is fighting a hard battle.

— JOHN WATSON

WE DON'T KNOW WHAT CHALLENGES FACE THE PEOPLE we meet each day. Is the bald woman in the movie theater a skinhead, or is she battling cancer? Is the beautiful woman with the storybook marriage dealing with her husband's adultery, while battling bulimia, as Princess Diana turned out to be? Is the woman on the airplane with the crying infant going home to her own mother's funeral? Is the man in the speeding red car weaving in and out of traffic on his way to the hospital with his toddler who swallowed cleaning fluid? These are just a few reminders that situations are not always as they appear.

> *You have the power to bring someone hope, if only for a moment. And that hope can multiply a thousand times.*

Why not give others the benefit of the doubt since chances are you don't know the whole story. Above all, be kind. You have the power to bring someone hope, if only for a moment. And that hope can multiply a thousand times. And who knows? It could come back to someone you love.

THE DAYMAKER SMILE

The way you look at others,
your smile, and your small acts of caring
can create happiness.

— THICH NHAT HANH

THE DAYMAKER IS EASILY SPOTTED because her smile is not fleeting or forced, but relaxed and genuine. To be a Daymaker, you simply have to serve others unreservedly. When you do, your smile comes naturally, and it's the kind of smile that touches something in every one of us.

There is nothing better than a great big, unsolicited, natural smile—whether you're offering it or receiving it.

SMILE AND SAY HELLO TO STRANGERS

Be not forgetful to entertain strangers:
for thereby some have entertained angels unawares.

— HEBREWS 13:2

WHEN MY DAUGHTERS AND I GO FOR A WALK in our neighborhood, I tell them we will wave to everyone we see and wish them a good day. When you do this with a five-year-old and a two-year-old, everyone smiles and says, "Thank you." Some shake my kids hands and some have even hugged them. When I do this on my own, people seem entertained, amused, or sometimes a little puzzled. I have not gotten a hug yet, but I keep hoping.

SURPRISE PEOPLE WITH YOUR GREAT ATTITUDE

Cheerfulness, like spring,
opens all the blossoms
of the inward man.

— JEAN PAUL RICHTER

RECENTLY I WAS WAITING FOR A FLIGHT AT AN AIRPORT, when an announcement informed us the flight was cancelled. Not surprisingly, I was frustrated. I needed to call home to let my wife know I'd be late and I was concerned about the possibility of not getting on the next flight. A little while later I was again near the gate when a gentleman with a big smile on his face approached the counter to check-in. Upon hearing the flight was cancelled, he looked at the stressed-out airline employee and said, "No problem, absolutely no problem. I know it's not your fault, is there anything I can do to help make your job easier this evening?" The employee's mouth dropped open. She had been alone for quite a while dealing with the rage of a long line of customers, including myself. This Daymaker didn't let it bother him, and even wanted to help. He gave her some perspective and reminded the rest of us that there was a better way to handle it.

SMALL KINDNESSES THAT MAKE SOMEONE'S DAY

No act of kindness, no matter how small,
is ever wasted.

— AESOP

IF YOU HAVE A NICE THOUGHT ABOUT SOMEONE, go ahead and tell them. We often look at others, have a nice thought about them, and fail to say anything. Why keep it to yourself? If you like someone's outfit, hairstyle, voice, or another attribute, share it with them. However, you should draw the line at physique. That enters a personal area they might not find so complimentary.

Let people merge into traffic. Why is it that when you let someone merge onto the highway, they turn and wave to thank you? Probably because it is so rare these days. Everyone is in such a hurry to get to work, school, soccer practice, or home that the road has become a competition to get ahead of others, instead of an opportunity to make someone's day by letting them merge in front of us. Are we in such a hurry that we can't show up for work one car length later? If you let more than one person in at a time, however, it doesn't make the day for the person behind you. You can be a Daymaker and still be practical.

If you have a nice thought about someone, go ahead and tell them.

Tip the taxi driver. On one of my first trips to New York, I stayed at the Waldorf-Astoria. One morning I had a business meeting at an address I didn't know well, so I asked the doorman to get me a cab. As the cab pulled away from the hotel I told the driver the address. He went nuts. "Are you crazy? That's a block and a half away!" He was so upset and I felt like such a tourist. I decided to make his day, so I gave him twenty dollars and told him to keep the change. He looked back at me and smiled. "Thank you. I was waiting in that line for a half an hour. Now I can go home and enjoy my family."

Stop for people with a flat tire. My wife's Uncle Floyd told me a great story of one cold winter night when he came upon a car with a flat tire. It was in the middle of the country, here in Minnesota, which gives a whole new meaning to the word cold. The driver was an elderly lady obviously incapable of changing the tire. So Uncle Floyd proceeded to do it, freezing his butt off in the process. When he finished the job, she opened her purse to pay him. He didn't want any money for helping her, but she insisted. Then she pulled out a quarter and a dime, placing it gently in his hand. To him it was worth more than a hundred-dollar bill.

Tip as much as you can. Even if it's only a little, leave something. It will make your day as much as the recipient's. The following story illustrates this:

In the days, when an ice cream sundae cost much less than they do now, a 10-year-old boy entered a coffee shop and sat down at a table. When the waitress put a glass of water in front of him he asked, "How much is an ice cream sundae?"

"Fifty cents," replied the waitress. The little boy pulled his hand out of his pocket and studied the coins in it. "Well, how much is a plain dish of ice cream?" he inquired. By now, other people were waiting for tables and the waitress was growing impatient. "Thirty-five cents," she brusquely replied. The little boy again counted his coins. "I'll have the plain ice cream," he said. The waitress brought the ice cream, put the bill on the table and walked away. The boy finished the ice cream, paid the cashier and left.

When the waitress came back to wipe down the table, she began to cry. There, placed neatly beside the empty dish, were two nickels and five pennies. You see he couldn't afford the sundae, because he needed to have enough left over to give her a tip.

THE DAYMAKER TRAVELER

> *Though we travel the world over to find the beautiful,*
> *we must carry it with us or we find it not.*
>
> — RALPH WALDO EMERSON

AT JUUT, we try to model ourselves after other admirable businesses. One company that I had heard about for years is Southwest Airlines, and its CEO Herb Kelleher. It's a no frills operation with inexpensive rates. What attracts a lot of attention is the playful staff. I decided to see what all the hoopla was about.

I needed to attend a conference in Orlando and then go to New Orleans on business the next day, so for that leg of my trip I booked a flight on Southwest.

At the airport gate I received a boarding card. To speed up departures, they give no one a seat. The earlier you arrive, the earlier you board. My colleague and I had our choice of seats in the middle, and made ourselves comfortable.

The pilot riddled his P.A. announcements with humor as we taxied down the runway. The flight attendants smiled and treated the passengers with an easy camaraderie. Here we sat in coach, having a ball, all because of the employees of this extraordinary airline. They made us feel not only appreciated, but also an important part of their day. I loved Southwest because they practiced their own brand of Daymaking.

A MERE EIGHT HOURS LATER …

Where one will not,
two cannot quarrel.

— SPANISH PROVERB

WITH MY BUSINESS IN NEW ORLEANS FINISHED, I boarded the major carrier that services the Minneapolis/St. Paul area. Because I had so many frequent flyer miles, I was flying first class. In first class, they hang your jacket when you board, so I picked up a magazine and left my coat draped over the seat. I became so engrossed in my magazine that I didn't notice the flight attendant slide my coat off the armrest. She glared at me clearly upset about something. I still hadn't realized she had taken my jacket, when a few minutes later she asked the gentlemen ahead of me if he would like anything to drink.

"A glass of red wine please," he replied and then thanked her.

"Thank *you*. Not everyone is so nice as you to say thank you," she said, again glaring at me.

What did I do? I wondered.

"Man, she's brutal to you tonight," the man next to me commented.

It seemed pretty ironic that earlier in the day I had a great time flying coach, and now I was sitting in first class feeling miserable. I needed to do something to remedy the situation.

So when the flight attendant came around again, I caught her attention. "I'm sorry if I was inattentive during takeoff," I apologized. "I was in the middle of an article in my magazine. Could we start over by my telling you how much I appreciate you taking such good care of us this evening?" She gave me a sheepish, but appreciative smile. This ended the tension of my flight home. We all felt better. I know it made my day.

ALLOW SOMEONE IN LINE TO GO AHEAD OF YOU

If you want others to be happy, practice compassion.
If you want to be happy, practice compassion.

DALAI LAMA

NOTICE PEOPLE WHO ARE LATE for their planes at check-in. You could change the course of their day by letting them go in front of you. A fellow traveler with only one bag would greatly appreciate you letting him ahead of you, your family, and your 12 pieces of luggage. It's also kind to let someone with a connecting flight jump ahead on the plane, so they don't miss their next plane. The same concept applies to letting someone with just a couple of items in front of your full basket at the grocery store.

> *Be kind, rewind, and remember to smile with love.*

You have many opportunities to make a strangers' day, whether it's politely declining the telemarketer on the phone instead of just hanging up, or tipping the bagger who helps you to the car at the grocery store. Be kind, rewind, and remember to smile with love.

CHAPTER EIGHT

A Company of Daymakers

To be good is noble;
but to show others how to be good
is nobler and no trouble.

— MARK TWAIN

W ORK SHOULD BE AN EXPRESSION of who you are, a personal calling. Your work is a big part of your purpose on earth. You know someone is suited to her job when she loves to do it and does it well. I have been offering seminars on Daymaking for over 15 years now and I'm still amazed at how positively people respond. Many have taken the concept back to their own companies and created a renewed sense of purpose in their work place. The range of businesses varies from little coffee shops, retail stores, and medical clinics to financial services, car dealerships, and major banks. All of them see the value of Daymaking, not only to their customers or patients but to their employees as well. Having a sense of purpose in your work, whether you're saving a life or making someone's coffee, is truly a blessing. Companies have initiated Daymaker of the Week contests, have given Daymaker awards away, have created Daymaker storybooks at work, and more.

Every few weeks I get another business card with the title Daymaker on it. To see this idea spreading around the globe is gratitfying. I have gotten cards from Taiwan, Singapore, Germany, Italy, and India. The word continues to spread in a variety of ways and to see people from various walks of life, vocations, occupations, and nationalities gravitate to being Daymakers gives me hope for the future. Corporate CEOs in conservative business suits, as well as 19-year-olds with multiple body piercings, can all share in the Daymaking phenomenon. That in itself is extraordinary.

A COMPANY MISSION OF MAKING CUSTOMERS' DAYS

Give the world the best you have
and the best will come back to you.

— MADELINE BRIDGES

YOUR MISSION STATEMENT IS A PROMISE to your customer. Keeping that promise is the most important part of a business. It's easy to write a lofty mission statement, but making it the living reality of your company tests your commitment to it.

At Juut, customer service has expanded beyond just providing commodities in a friendly, efficient manner. We fulfill customers' haircut, color, and spa treatment needs, but we also strive to surprise, amuse, and educate them in entertaining ways. A number of years ago we wanted to know how we could better serve our clients so, we began asking them to fill out a simple survey with three questions:

- ✳ What did you like most? The overwhelming answer: the staff.
- ✳ What did you like least? The overwhelming answer: waiting.
- ✳ What would you like done differently next time?

The answers vary from better music, less time on hold, to boxed lunches to go.

Clients' expectations change with each visit, but what they like most continues to be our staff.

I believe that anyone who has chosen to serve others is in an enviable position, if they approach what they do as a gift. I also believe that those who serve with the most sincerity possess what I call "servant's hearts." That doesn't mean we're inferior, but rather that we're in a unique position to make their day. You could say that we have a noble purpose.

What is your noble purpose in going to work? Does the company you work for have one? Do your coworkers share in it? Work is so much more fulfilling when you know that what you are doing may have a profound effect on someone else's day or life. And remember, that holds true whether you're the President of the United States or a barrista serving coffee at Starbucks.

So, if you're not clear on how your work contributes to the world around you, take a look at your company's mission statement. Many times they convey a noble purpose. I believe company mission statements should be short enough to fit on a bumper sticker. They should also be clear and meaningful. An organization only becomes successful when its mission statement is based on values that are also important to employees and to customers. At Juut, our noble purpose, our reason for being, is simple: **We Serve and Replenish.**

> *An organization only becomes successful when its mission statement is based on values that are also important to employees and to customers.*

We get out of bed in the morning excited because every day we serve around 4,000 guests in our salons, spas, and stores. By replenishing them, we create an amazing ripple effect in our communities.

Our staff understands this ripple effect and their role in it. When I ask them why they work at Juut, they tell me it's because of the mission: to serve and replenish. People don't lead, purpose does. Noble purpose is profound in its simplicity. It is the essence of why you do what you do, and why your company exists. You can have an incredible career as a Daymaker doing any type of job, as long as you serve others. Think of all the opportunities you have throughout the day to touch people.

Being a hairstylist taught me that many people hunger for genuine relationships. With the fast pace of life that many people lead, they simply don't take the time to foster relationships outside their family and/or work environment. Consequently they miss out on important human connections. From time to time everyone needs an ear to listen, a shoulder to cry on, or a person with whom to share a genuine Daymaker smile. Whether it is with your hairstylist, mail carrier, neighbor, or a relative. So take the time to listen, and share with those who seek you out. Then, when you really need someone, they will be there for you.

> *Take the time to listen, and share with those who seek you out. Then, when you really need someone, they will be there for you.*

I have had the opportunity to follow some of my clients through high school, college, marriage, and children. We've been through good times and also some traumatic times. I value each of them and enjoy playing some small role in their lives. I have traveled out of town for my clients' weddings when it wasn't about doing her hair; it was about sharing in the happiness of the day. I have had clients give me incredibly personal mementos; videos of their wedding, pictures from trips, even video footage of a childbirth! Once, I was even asked if I would videotape one of my client's deliveries for her. I politely declined. It does go to show how connected people get with the person who has listened, cared, and repeatedly made his or her day. It instills a trust that still inspires me.

Our goal at Juut is to create strong, long-term relationships and loyalty with customers. So the management starts by forming close ties with our staff. The leadership team provides employees with education, financial planning, goal setting, coaching, marketing, and a nurturing environment. Caring for our employees gives them the skill and inspiration to replenish our external customer, the clients. Surpassing the needs and expectations of our staff gives them the energy and motivation to serve clients in unexpected and genuine ways. As a company, we fill people up with love and joy, from management's relationship with each staff member to their relationships with each other, and finally to the relationships they have with clients. Clients want to do business with a company that takes care of its employees.

As one retail adviser told me, "I can work all day, and when I start to get tired, I just think about how I can help that [client] in front of me. Daymaking has motivated and inspired me to believe in myself. I feel like I am not the only one who cares, who loves, and thinks about others." Having the goal of truly caring for the people they serve can motivate workers to go the extra mile.

You can make a customer's day in big or small ways. A massage therapist at Juut told me the following:

* My clients come to me feeling weary, overused, and distant. I help them to get in touch with themselves physically, which often brings up emotions inside them.

✳ Many people cry in my dimly-lit room and share stories of heart-break and courage. These people are all Daymakers to someone: teachers, who deserve more thanks, nurses, who go day after day to a job fraught with emotional peril. Firemen have cried in the peaceful safety of my room of those [they have] lost. I have had a nervous bride or groom before their wedding day and a pregnant woman anticipating birth and parenthood. We are all Daymakers. People leave me ready to serve others [after] having been refilled themselves. Kindness can change a person's life as much as tragedy.

At Juut, to serve and replenish is our brand, our promise to our customers. Other companies have noble purposes, as well. Some have found inspiration directly from Juut. Gary Edelston, RFC, Senior Vice President, Wealth Enhancement Group, said the following:

We have begun to initiate "Daymaker" types of changes into our organization. Immediately, we noticed how willing and excited our employees embraced the philosophy. We have more to do, but at least in our small part of the world, we are gentler, our employees are happier, and the lives of all of those we touch are better.

HELP PEOPLE REFINE THEIR IDEA OF SUCCESS

*True greatness consists in being great
in the little things.*

— CHARLES SIMMONS

A FEW YEARS AGO, we hired a young woman from a very small town to work as an assistant in one of our salons. In this role, customers found her wholesome and refreshing. But I knew that once she became a stylist, clients would want more sophistication to feel they could trust her with their images.

When she graduated from her apprenticeship and prepared to take on her own clientele, I took her out to a fine restaurant to show her how they served high-expectation clients. As I walked into the restaurant I spotted her in what looked like a prom dress. The maître d' led us to our table, pulled out her chair, unfolded her napkin, and laid it on her lap. She didn't know how to react. Then the waiter described the day's specials with passionate expertise. She didn't recognize anything on the menu and wasn't even sure what to drink. She asked me what I liked. "Well, the caprese salad and the risotto are my favorites," I told her. "And they have a wonderful Merlot by the glass."

"That's what I'll have," she said with relief. Halfway though the meal, she excused herself to go to the ladies room. While she was gone, the waiter folded her napkin and pushed in her chair. When she returned, he pulled her chair out and unfolded her napkin to place in her lap again. We had a delicious meal and talked about client expectations and the behind-the-chair etiquette in our salon.

At work the next day this woman blew me away. Overnight, this small town girl had adopted the elegance and attentiveness she had experienced the night before. Her voice had softened and her body moved with regal skill. She turned the chair gently; emulating the gracious way the waiter had pulled hers out. She unfolded her cutting cape like he had unfolded her napkin. Her ability to serve customers accustomed to impeccable service came from receiving that level of service herself.

A COMPANY CULTURE OF MAKING EACH OTHER'S DAYS

All altruism springs from putting yourself
in the other person's place

— HARRY EMERSON FOSDICK

WITH MORE STAFF MEMBERS THAN MANAGERS, workers themselves have a far bigger impact on each other than anyone has on them. Sharing the company vision often helps make our noble purpose a part of employees' daily lives. We know we have been successful when our staff enthusiastically helps each other. Here are some ideas for making your coworkers day:

* Take each other out for lunch on birthdays.
* If you read a good book bring it in and give it to someone you think would also enjoy it.
* Know their children's names.
* Write thank you notes when you think they did a good job, a customer complimented them, or they made your day.

- Pass around birthday cards, get well cards, and anniversary of their job cards for everyone to sign.
- Bring them coffee, tea, or some other little treat.
- If they are swamped with work, offer to pick up some lunch for them.
- Smile and be happy to see them. We all feel uplifted by people who like us.
- If you need to correct any error or behavior, do it in a gentle, kind way that tells them that while they made a mistake, you still like them and believe in them.

A COMPANY COMMITMENT OF MAKING EMPLOYEES' DAYS

We make a living by what we get,
but we make a life by what we give.

— NORMAN MACEWAN

BY MAKING EMPLOYEES FEEL SPECIAL AND CARED FOR, you inspire them to treat others that way. Here are some ways to make your staff's days.

Pass a Bouquet

Each week bring a bouquet of flowers to work and give it to someone who made your day recently. Then, have the person who receives it pass it on the next day to someone who has made their day and so on. When the week is up, five people have been told in a beautiful, tangible way, thank you for making my day. Recognition is a great motivator.

Daymaker Cards

We have cards in our break rooms that staff members can fill out to recognize someone who has made their day by helping out or complimenting them. We post these cards on the bulletin board in the break room for everyone to see. We also read them in our team meetings to acknowledge the value of Daymaking in big and small ways at work. It makes my day to give and receive them.

Know Each Employee's Favorite Flower

Less of something special is better than more of something ordinary. Each of our employee's files indicates his or her favorite flower. Periodically, we send a note of congratulations for a promotion, engagement, pregnancy, and other events, as well as our sympathies for a loss of a loved one or an injury. Instead of sending them a bouquet, we send them one stem of their favorite flower. Imagine getting one beautiful, fragrant stem of freesia with a note vs. an average bouquet. That goes for other gifts as well. One employee might enjoy theater tickets while another would prefer to go to the zoo with their kids. Personalize gifts to the individual.

Harmony Awards

Each year at Juut, we have an Annual Summit where we recognize high sales, anniversaries, and other significant events. The most coveted awards are what we call the Harmony Awards. Each salon votes for an individual who has brought the most harmony to their workplace that year. We compile the comments and recognize them in front of the whole company. Tears of joy flow, not only from recipients, but from their coworkers as well. When you place value on such things as harmony in the workplace that is what you get.

Make Their Wild Ideas Come True

My employees help me achieve my wild idea of having a great company doing great things, and part of having a great company is helping employees realize their wild ideas.

I ask our employees to share their wild ideas, and then Juut provides resources for them to experience as many as possible. Some of our employees want to buy a house, so we give classes on buying a first home. Some want to go to Europe to study, so we arrange tours. Some want to open their own salons, so we also offer classes on that. It might seem idiotic to teach your staff how to become your competition, but I don't see it that way. We teach them the pros and the cons, the risks and the rewards, and at the end of the day most find that they enjoy continuing as employees of Juut.

> *When you place value on such things as harmony in the workplace that is what you get.*

Those who do decide to open a salon have a much better understanding of what it takes, and I believe we have an "emotional bank account" with these individuals.

They learn not to steal staff from ours or other businesses, because it will come back to them one day. Some have left to open their own salons and have done so with great integrity.

Those who share their wild ideas give themselves an advantage. One of our staff dreamed of doing hair for *Vogue* magazine. About a year after he shared his idea with me, Vogue called asking me to do the hair for an upcoming photo shoot in Minneapolis. I told them I had someone perfect for the job. My employee couldn't believe his wild idea would come true. The shoot was spectacular. Some of the other employees felt upset that they didn't get to do the shoot. I told them if I'd known it was their wild idea, I would have considered them for it. Now people constantly tell me their wild ideas.

My wild idea has become helping others realize theirs, and it's enormously rewarding. Remember the last line of the poem, *Beauty Tips* by Sam Levenson, mentioned earlier: *As you grow older you will discover you have two hands, one for helping yourself and one for helping others.*

LEADERS SHOULD BE LIFELONG STUDENTS

People never improve
unless they look to some standard or example
higher and better than themselves.

— TYRON EDWARDS

WHAT DO DAYMAKING AND LEADERSHIP have in common? You must have a Daymaker's heart and a Daymaker's intuition about people to be a great leader. This is true, whether you are a teacher, hairstylist, or leader of a country or a charitable program. The talents and skills needed to lead are similar no matter the circumstance.

I had the fortunate experience of being mentored by many outstanding leaders both in and outside the beauty industry. One of my favorite experiences was studying under Dr. Edward Deming, the father of the Quality Uniformity Movement whose methods revolutionized Japanese manufacturing in the 1950s, and were later embraced by the United States in the 1980s. What I learned about systems and true quality could fill a whole book. He taught me things I will never forget and I am forever in his gratitude. The first time we met, he was in his late 80s, doing a seminar on systems in business. He asked the audience what types of business and industry they represented. After a few responded: IBM, Raytheon, 3M, etc., I stood up and said, "Hairdressing." He paused and rose from his chair and looked at me in puzzlement. Then he said, "Well, that's a first. Nothing wrong with it. It's just a first."

Not knowing what you don't know is a common condition that can hold you back. Get out there and learn! Be a student of life. Education keeps you fresh, interested, and interesting. At Juut we call this Lifelong Learning. I recommend that my entire staff of Daymakers take classes regularly. Whether it's a business-building class, advanced biology, pottery, or yoga, learning something new expands your mind and nourishes your soul.

SHARE YOUR SUCCESS

Leadership means not giving orders to others,
but giving of yourself.

— EAST AFRICAN TRIBAL PROVERB

A LEADER has two important characteristics. First, you've got to show that you're going somewhere and second, you have to be able to persuade other people to go with you. Leadership is the art of getting others to want to do something you are convinced needs to be done. Creating a successful company is easy: ask others to take on important responsibilities, encourage them to do it as well as possible, and then give them all the credit. When you give the accolades away, you don't get acknowledged for your part. Instead, you have the satisfaction of creating leaders. This becomes a powerful chain reaction. Take pride in sharing success and you will have more success to share.

VALIDATE EACH STEP OF GROWTH

Men must walk,
at least,
before they dance.

— ALEXANDER POPE

ANOTHER CRUCIAL PIECE OF DAYMAKING is to praise people, even if they haven't yet done things perfectly. It's like having a one-year-old who just learned to walk. If

I waited to praise my daughter until she walked perfectly, how motivated would she be? I wouldn't enjoy sitting around hoping she would finally walk perfectly.

Acknowledge any improvement, no matter how small. A pat on the back from the boss always makes the staff's days and keeps them motivated to do more. I must confess that this lesson did not come easily to me. I had a very hard time praising mediocrity, yet all the managers asked that I please let the staff know they were doing a good job. Then one day it occurred to me that with our high standards, people who were mediocre in our company, would be star players elsewhere. When I started to appreciate the small stuff, it had big results.

> *Acknowledge any improvement, no matter how small.*

Find ways to convince your people that you see them all as either winners or potential winners and you're there to support them. In all of the mentoring I've received, I always felt like a winner. In many instances, this gave me the confidence to actually respond to a situation as a leader, not someone who was trying to become one.

We solicit input from staff because they know their job best. The closer you get to the front line, where most of the action occurs, the more employee input is necessary. At Juut, we provide our team members with a "How Are We Doing This Month?" survey. They are given the opportunity to comment, make suggestions, gripe, or praise all the various aspects of the company, (i.e. marketing, front desk, education, etc.) We have gotten very useful feedback and implemented many of the ideas. Always ask people on the front line. That's where you'll get the real answers.

BRILLIANT MANAGEMENT LEAVES ROOM FOR INSPIRATION

Power can be seen as
power with rather than power over,
and it can be used for competence and cooperation,
rather than dominance and control.

— ANNE L. BARSTOW

MANAGEMENT AND GREAT LEADERSHIP are two different things. Management must efficiently oversee logistical details like placing orders, paying the bills on time, ensuring paychecks are correct, and following regulations. Leaders, on the other hand, must steer the boat and chart new courses when necessary, which can be quite dramatic. If you have a business that is poorly managed, the drama plays out as crisis control. Orders not on time, inventory too low, union strikes, and other administrative issues cause negative drama. People get upset, misinformation travels through the group, and workers worry about basic issues. High sales, great performance, exceptional teamwork, and profits are the right kind of drama.

Leadership must also react to issues appropriately. Handling problems is an art. Some managers overreact even to small obstacles. I've heard this called pole-vaulting over mouse poop. Some leaders make big issues out of nothing. I have never been on a flight where the pilot announces to the passengers that the plane is off course, yet planes are off course over 90 percent of the time. Passing on each difficulty would only add to everyone's stress and erode trust in the pilot's abilities. Instead of reacting with fear and blame to every situation, respond calmly and efficiently. It will make things easier and you will get better results from a staff that is not paralyzed by panic.

Leadership is about stability, security, and growth. If you own a sports franchise that is managed poorly, the drama will probably be issues such as player holdouts, dissatisfied fans, and threats about moving the team. While during a winning season the drama usually happens in the game, not in front office issues. Many companies experience the same thing. Some airlines seem to always have labor negotiations. Service suffers because morale is poor. The drama centers on whether they will strike or enact a slowdown, not their on-time arrivals and high customer service levels.

We do everything we can in our company to celebrate service, productivity and staff growth. We try to keep daily operations as predictable as possible. Systems that create stability allow you to focus on making the business better instead of cleaning up messes.

CREATE LEADERS

> *Trust men and they will be true to you;*
> *treat them greatly and they will*
> *show themselves great.*
>
> — RALPH WALDO EMERSON

A LEADER NEEDS TO SEE OPPORTUNITIES ahead of the competition, and also keep danger away. This ability comes from experience and keen awareness. The more opportunity that you provide people and the more you protect them from danger, the more respect they give you. Having gained their respect, you can move into a position of power.

When I move someone in our organization into a leadership position, I orchestrate it so they can gain respect first. This sets them up to succeed. They don't have to earn trust, loyalty, and respect from their staff while they learn their new job.

Bringing outsiders in is difficult unless you gain respect from the group first based on your endorsement and confidence in them. Then the new person will be better received. But the outsider still needs to exhibit leadership abilities to earn respect on their own. Once you have a position of power it's important never to misuse or abuse it. Using power for positive change and encouraging others, while never misusing that power, is my personal quest as a leader.

Calvin Coolidge was invited to a dinner hosted by Dwight Morrow, the father of Anne Morrow Lindbergh. After Coolidge had excused himself for the evening, Morrow expressed his belief that Coolidge would make a good president. The others disagreed and a heated discussion ensued concerning Coolidge's qualifications. Those who didn't believe in his presidential potential felt he was too quiet, lacking charisma, and personality. He just wasn't likable enough, they said.

> *Using power for positive change and encouraging others, while never misusing that power.*

"I like him," commented Anne, then age six. Displaying a finger with a bandage around it, she continued, "He was the only one at the party who asked about my sore finger, and that's why he would make a good president."

Anne had a good point. In order to lead, one has to have sincerity, a spirit of kindness, and a genuine concern for others.

A Daymaking company makes kindness and generosity an integrated part of its every activity. With this kind of ideal pervading the culture, employees feel inspired and excited about giving more than they ever thought they could. This results in incredible customer service, fulfilled staff members, and a win/win result for everyone.

CHAPTER NINE

Change the World
by Making One Day at a Time

When you rise in the morning,
form a resolution to make the day
a happy one for a fellow creature.

— SYDNEY SMITH

E ACH OF US CAN MAKE A DIFFERENCE in the world. For me, inspiring just one person to become kinder and more loving will make writing this book worth it. Making other people feel cared for is the greatest power we have. We all have that power every day as we move through our lives. Listening to someone having a rough day, smiling at a stranger, and waving at a toddler are the kind of small things we can do to make this a more positive world. As you go through every day taking care of your responsibilities, notice how many times you have a chance to be kind instead of acting impatient or indifferent to others. A little friendliness and caring from you will make life easier for everyone you meet. Doing this will change your life.

A Community of Daymakers

Think globally, act locally.

— Bumper sticker

As we become Daymakers in different parts of our lives, it is natural to want to reach out and help more people in our community. Many people donate money or used items, volunteer for charitable organizations, help in hospitals, join their church in doing good works for the less fortunate, take part in charity drives, and any number of other benevolent activities. When we make a splash in someone else's life, it starts a chain reaction. We give them joy and hope that then moves out into their own lives. As they touch more people, our splash becomes a bigger wave, creating the ripple effect of waves moving out in many directions through all of the people who are subsequently touched.

My volunteer work has taught me so much and helped me gain a perspective on what is most important in life. No matter what your talents and interests, there are many places where you can give your services.

DAYMAKING VOLUNTEERS

You have not lived a perfect day
even though you have earned your money,
unless you have done something for someone
who will never be able to repay you.

— RUTH SMELTZER

MOST PEOPLE HAVE THE DESIRE to help those less fortunate, but don't know the best way to go about doing it. At Juut we provide our staff with the opportunity to volunteer. We set up programs that allow our Daymakers to give their time easily on a regular basis. The most amazing part is that the employees who resisted volunteering the most have become our most enthusiastic participants. Once they have a taste of how good it feels to give to strangers who need them, they want to do it as much as possible.

Help the Homeless

Frederic Holzberger, whose company owns a beauty school and several Aveda stores, is the Aveda distributor in Ohio, Kentucky, Michigan, and Indiana. He has created his own special program for homeless people. A number of years ago, I did a seminar for his company and discussed making people's days. Frederic was then inspired to start an organization called Project Daymaker. He converted a Winnebago motor home into a hair salon to serve homeless people. He and his staff drive this motor home to different locations throughout his territory, and enlist salons that are customers of his to volunteer their services for people in transition. Many of these individuals have their hair done for job interviews, or just to feel better about themselves. Many of them have never received a professional salon treatment before, and it really makes their days. They laugh and smile radiantly as the volunteers take care of them. Project Daymaker also inspires the people providing the services, as their hearts become filled with love and caring.

Most people want to volunteer, but seldom take action. It takes leaders like Frederic to provide a program like Project Daymaker to allow it to happen.

Benefit a Children's Hospital

Families facing a child with an acute illness have days plagued with worry, stress, and heartache. In these environments their every waking moment can become consumed with the uncertainty of their situation. While we cannot wipe away the crisis for them, we can give them a much-needed reprieve by either helping the child or the parents. Juut provides haircuts, manicures, foot massages, and other services for the children. Our staff members also spend time just hanging out with them having fun. We provide the same services for the parents of kids with cancer who are staying at the Ronald McDonald house in Minneapolis. What can we do for the parents? Mow their lawn, wash their car, or cook them dinner.

There are all kinds of opportunities to make both a child's and the parent's days. One of our most successful programs involves holding and cuddling new-born babies. We train our volunteers in infant massage. Giving love to a child, who so desperately needs it, reminds us all of what's most important in life. When you fulfill such a deep need, you know that your actions truly make a difference.

DAYMAKING TEENS: KIDS CAN MAKE A DIFFERENCE TOO

Children are the living messages
we send to a time we will not see.

— NEIL POSTMAN, *THE DISAPPEARANCE OF CHILDHOOD*

FOR THE LAST SEVEN YEARS, I HAVE VOLUNTEERED as a guest speaker at a local Minnesota high school. I made the commitment to give back to my community, but what I have taught these students pales in comparison to what I have learned from them. I hadn't been in a high school since graduating in 1977, so I felt a bit nervous facing four classes of 30 kids each. Though businesses that pay a lot of money to hear me speak have high expectations, I figured teenagers would be my most difficult audience yet. I had bought into the media's portrayal of teens as apathetic and lazy. However, I found that today's youth are really no different than when I was in school. Sure the clothes and music have changed, but these kids have optimism about the future that surprised me.

From the first day I spoke with them, the students connected with the Daymaker concept. They not only listened intently, but also enthusiastically brainstormed about various possibilities. Their ability to mobilize and take action delighted me the most. These 120 teenagers started a Project Daymaker in their school with the goal that every one of them would touch ten other students a day. They wanted each of the 1000 students in that school to benefit from Daymaking. Here are just a few of the ideas they put into action:

One day a student put Starburst candies with Daymaker notes on all the cars in the parking lot.

A teacher received a flower and an anonymous note while I was in his class. He told the class that this was a first in his over 30 years of teaching.

The students honored a few teachers about to retire by passing a book around in which students could write notes of appreciation. The last week of school they gave them to the teachers, their own *Mr. Holland's Opus.*

The students shared Daymaking with their parents by leaving notes of appreciation on their car windshields, and Post-it notes on their bathroom mirrors.

Several of these teenagers have also taken up community Daymaker projects, such as visiting senior citizens and reading to them.

"Most important is to always have the thought to be a true Daymaker," one student wrote me. "You throw off a certain vibe when you carry that attitude in your head. Then you can make someone's day by how you prevent yourself [from reacting negatively to situations]. You also see when someone else's day has been broken by another person . . . [and] try to do something to make their day."

This school and its students are determined to be Daymakers. They know that they can influence the legacy of their generation. One senior said to the class "Someday we are going to turn 30, and look back on our high school years and wonder what kind of mark we left." They do not want their generation remembered for Columbine-like tragedies. They are Daymakers who want to lift up each other, their hometown, and the rest of the world.

Teenagers have incredible energy and passion. With a little encouragement, they can create beautiful dreams to make the world a better place. By banding together, they can turn those dreams into a better world for all of us.

We all have so many ways we can make a better place, even outside our circle of family, friends, and work. Reaching out to help others in your community brings your life a greater sense of meaning and can bring you closer to family members, coworkers, or others who volunteer with you. Even devoting one day to a worthwhile organization can start to broaden the way you look at the world. The day you give will be a greater day for yourself and for the people whose day you make.

PASS KINDNESS ON TO EVERYONE YOU MEET

> *Nobody makes a greater mistake*
> *than he who did nothing*
> *because he could only do a little.*
>
> — EDMUND BURKE

YOU CAN REACH OUT TO OTHERS in more situations than you realize. One night I sat working on my book in a booth at Mama's Fish House in Paia, Hawaii when a waitress just finishing her shift stood nearby wondering if she should splurge on a glass of wine. She had a tough day and had not made much money. Watching her with her customers and coworkers that evening, I had recognized a fellow Daymaker, so I asked her what wine she liked and ordered her a glass. I told her about my book on making people's days. Her coworker Chris joined our discussion.

You can reach out to others in more situations than you realize.

The two of them told me about the corporate jobs they had given up on the mainland for this simple, peaceful life in Paia. They both had family back home that didn't understand why they wasted their college degrees waiting tables in Maui. Both said they would now tell their families they were Daymakers. Chris became so inspired that the next day he stayed late to cover one of his coworker's shifts, when she suddenly needed to leave early. It made her day, and his.

A few months later Chris sent me this poem:

A message brought, begins to spread.
As through your words, old fears are shed.
For the thoughts of one will soon migrate, when willing minds do congregate.
A joy in me does reawake, when through my smile, your day I make.
Keep up the great work.

You never know when or where you will have a chance to open someone's mind to life as a Daymaker.

THE DAYMAKER WARRIOR

Everybody can be great, because anybody can serve.
You only need a heart full of grace.

— MARTIN LUTHER KING, JR.

I USED TO FIND MYSELF SITTING ON THE SIDELINES of life and hoping the world would somehow become better. But just wishing doesn't help. Now I realize I must actively be the change I want to see in the world.

My life's work is to serve others, and influence them to do the same. I feel like a Daymaker warrior. This means that no matter what I face each day, I remain determined to find a way to bring joy and hope to people around me. I focus on having calmness, compassion, humor, and a positive attitude.

We can take comfort in looking back at the end of our lives to recall how many people we have touched in positive ways. How happy we will feel that we have led productive lives full of love and joy. It would be a tragedy not to be able to look back on our lives with pride and satisfaction. What we experience is up to us. We cannot change the past and the mistakes we have made, but we can learn from them and make the most of each day ahead.

Have an extraordinary life by making the days of everyone you touch. Act out of concern for others. As you do this more often, you will develop the habit of Daymaking. You will think less of your own concerns and more of the impact you can have on another's day. You will find peace and joy. Kindness will become effortless and unconscious. It will become who you are. You will fill your life with perfect moments.

THE DAYMAKER REVOLUTION: MY WILDEST IDEA YET

If one is lucky,
a solitary fantasy can
totally transform one million realities.

— MAYA ANGELOU

AS MY STORY DEMONSTRATES, you don't need a master's degree or a doctorate to make the world a better place. I have knowledge that does not come from a formal education, just many experiences that have taught me on a soul level. I am part of a revolution of inspired people who see the opportunity to change the world simply by making other people's days.

While some lament the state of the world and fear what the future will bring, I see a planet on the brink of transformation. Many people are reevaluating their priorities. Millions work to create a better life for themselves and their loved ones. Personal growth, yoga, volunteer work, and charity have become powerful movements. Oprah Winfrey draws high ratings serving up "Change Your Life" TV that celebrates courageous and kind acts around the world, while teaching people how to heal themselves and deepen their relationships.

I believe that the world has more good than bad. Each of us has the ability to make the good bigger, while shrinking the bad. Kindness can inspire others. Kindness can diffuse anger. Kindness can bring hope, heal pain, and change the world.

When I became still, I became aware. I am aware that there is a tipping point in any circumstance, and that we are on the brink of one in the world today. I am also aware that I have a role, like you, in tipping it in the right direction. Why settle for a world full of fear, loneliness, despair, and hate? We cannot sit on the sidelines and hope things will change. Unfortunately, there are also forces pulling the opposite direction. I wrote this book because I believe a small group of people can change the world. I see it as a ripple effect. These good deeds become a drop in the water.

> *We can build a revolution of kindness, a guild of Daymakers in the world.*

I dream of a world for our children, and our children's children, in which this ripple has become a wave. It will become so powerful that it will wash away the unnecessary pain and suffering in the world. We can do this. We can build a revolution of kindness, a guild of Daymakers in the world. Join me on this path of changing the little things in life everyday. We'll see that these little deposits will result in a very large shift in our society in our lifetime. It's already happening.

I have a wild idea that this book can motivate people everywhere to make someone else's day. The world can change in our lifetimes. It starts with me, and with you. Help make this dream come true.

If this book has touched you, I ask you to pass it on to another "Daymaker in the making," and continue the ripple effect. Thank you for allowing me to share my life and dreams with you. I hope someday that we might meet and make each other's days.

Recommended Reading

Albion, Mark, *Making a Life, Making a Living: Reclaiming Your Purpose and Passion in Business and in Life*, New York: Warner Books, 2000.

Albom, Mitch, *Tuesdays with Morrie: An Old Man, A Young Man, and Life's Greatest Lesson*, New York: Doubleday, 1997.

Berry, Linda, *Internal Cleansing: Rid Your Body of Toxins and Return to Vibrant Good Health*, New York: Prima Publishing, 1997.

Coehlo, Paulo, *The Alchemist: A Fable About Following Your Dream*. Harper, San Francisco, 1993.

Covey, Stephen R., *The 7 Habits of Highly Successful Families: Building a Beautiful Family Culture in A Turbulent World*, New York: Golden Books, 1997

Dalai Lama, *Ethics for the New Millennium*, New York: Riverhead Books, 1999.

Dyer, Wayne, *Manifest Your Destiny: The Nine Spiritual Principles for Getting Everything You Want*, New York: Harper Collins, 1997.

Foundation for Inner Peace, *A Course in Miracles* 2nd revised edition, 1992.

Gegax, Tom, *Winning in the Game of Life: Self-Coaching Secrets for Success*, New York: Harmony Books, 1999.

Huang, Chungliang Al and Lynch, Jerry, *Thinking Body, Dancing Mind: Taosports for Extraordinary Performance in Athletics, Business, and Life*, New York: Bantam Books, 1994.

Kraftsow, Gary, *Yoga for Wellness: Healing with the Timeless Teachings of Viniyoga*, New York: Penguin Arkana, 1999.

Kushner, Harold S., *Living a Life That Matters: Resolving the Conflict Between Conscience and Success*, New York: Knopf, 2001.

Mandino, Og, *The Greatest Miracle in the World* (reissue), New York: Bantam Books, 1988.

Myss, Caroline, *Anatomy of the Spirit: The Seven Stages of Power and Healing*, New York: Harmony Books, 1996.

Rechelbacher, Horst, *Rejuvenation: A Wellness Guide for Women and Men*, New York: HarperCollins, 1987.

Rosenberg, Larry, *Breath by Breath: The Liberating Practice of Insight Meditation*, Boston: Shambala Publications, 1998.

Tolle, Eckhart, *The Power of Now: A Guide to Spiritual Enlightenment*, New World Library, 1999.

Turner, Kristina, *The Self-Healing Cookbook: A Macrobiotic Primer for Healing Body, Mind, and Moods with Whole Natural Foods*, 9th revised edition, Earthstone Press, 2002.

Vanzant, Iyanla, *One Day My Soul Just Opened Up: 40 Days and 40 Nights Toward Spiritual Strength and Personal Growth*, New York: Fireside, 1998.

Walsch, Neale Donald, *Conversations with God: An Uncommon Dialogue Book 1*, New York: Putnam, 1996.

Weil, Andrew, *Eight Weeks to Optimum Health: A Proven Program for Taking Full Advantage of Your Body's Natural Healing Power*, New York: Knopf, 1997.

Weisman, Arinna and Smith, Jean, *The Beginner's Guide to Insight Meditation*, New York: Bell Tower, 2001.

About David Wagner

D AVID WAGNER is a world-renowned hair stylist, artist, entrepreneur, educator, and "Daymaker." He is the Owner/Daymaker of Juut Salonspas, the original Aveda salons.

The word "Juut" means to refill and replenish, and David's salons do just that. In fact, this is where David has nurtured his concept of Daymaking for over 24 years. Collectively, the salons serve nearly 4000 customers everyday, and each of his 400 employees consider themselves personally responsible for making their clients' days. He deeply believes that if we make other people's happiness part of what makes us happy, we can then consciously begin to change the world. This is the heart of the Daymaking concept, and David's mission.

David began his career in the late 1970s as a student at the Horst Education Center (now the Aveda Institute) in Minneapolis, Minnesota. This began his long association with Horst Rechelbacher, founder and visionary of the beauty product giant, Aveda, and eventually led to collaboration in the Salon and Spa industry, until 1991 when David purchased Mr. Rechelbacher's Horst Salons to form his own Juut Salonspas.

David has taught his Daymaker concept to thousands all over the world, from high school students to business executives since 1986. His knowledge does not come from a formal education, just many experiences that have taught him on a soul level. He sees himself as part of a revolution of inspired people who see the opportunity to change the world simply by making another person's day. While some lament the state of the world and fear what the future will bring, David sees a planet on the brink of transformation. He believes that the world has more good than bad and that each of us has the ability to make the good bigger, while shrinking the bad. Kindness can inspire others, diffuse anger, bring hope, heal pain, and change the world.

David lives in Minnetrista, Minnesota, with his wife, Charlie, and their daughters, Coco and Ava.

Visit **www.daymakermovement.com** and learn more!

❋ Read about the other inspirational Daymaker stories from around the world.

❋ Watch David Wagner tell his own poignant Daymaker story.

❋ Share your own personal Daymaker stories.

❋ Purchase additional copies of the book to share with employees, friends, and coworkers and receive online discounts.

❋ Join the network of other Daymakers who will help support your personal mission.

Remember, it doesn't take much to create the ripple effect.
Let's continue to swing the pendulum in the direction
of caring, love, and contribution.

We hope this JODERE GROUP book has benefited you in your quest for personal, intellectual, and spiritual growth.

JODERE GROUP is passionate about bringing new and exciting books, such as *Life As a Daymaker,* to readers worldwide. Our company was created as a unique publishing and multimedia avenue for individuals whose mission it is to positively impact the lives of others. We recognize the strength of an original thought, a kind word and a selfless act—and the power of the individuals who possess them. We are committed to providing the support, passion, and creativity necessary for these individuals to achieve their goals and dreams.

JODERE GROUP is comprised of a dedicated and creative group of people who strive to provide the highest quality of books, audio programs, online services, and live events to people who pursue life-long learning. It is our personal and professional commitment to embrace our authors, speakers, and readers with helpfulness, respect, and enthusiasm.

For more information about our products, authors, or live events, please call (800) 569-1002 or visit us on the Web at **www.jodere.com**